# KALLIS' iBT TOEFL PATTERN

## Speaking 1

TOEFL® is a registered trademark of Educational Testing Services (ETS), Princeton, New Jersey, USA. The content in this text, including the practice prompts, Model Answer, and Hacking Strategy, is created and designed exclusively by KALLIS. This publication is not endorsed or approved by ETS.

**KALLIS' iBT TOEFL® Pattern** Speaking 1

**KALLIS EDU, INC.**
7490 Opportunity Road, Suite 203
San Diego, CA 92111
(858) 277-8600
info@kallisedu.com
www.kallisedu.com

Copyright © 2014 KALLIS EDU, INC.

All rights reserved. No part of this book may be reproduced, stored in a retrieval system, or transmitted in any form or by any means, electronic or mechanical, including photocopying, recording, or otherwise, without the prior written permission of the copyright owner.

**ISBN-10**: 1-5003-9099-2
**ISBN-13**: 978-1-5003-9099-0

**iBT TOEFL® Pattern - Speaking I** is the first of our three-level iBT TOEFL® Speaking Exam preparation book series.

Our **iBT TOEFL® Pattern Speaking** series simplifies each TOEFL speaking task into a series of simple steps, which ensures that students do not become overwhelmed as they develop their speaking skills. Moreover, our commitment to minimizing instruction and maximizing student practice assures that students have many opportunities to strengthen their speaking skills.

**KALLIS**

# KALLIS'

# TOEFL® iBT PATTERN
## SPEAKING 1
### FOUNDATION

# Getting Started

A study guide should familiarize the reader with the material found on the test, develop unique methods that can be used to solve various question types, and provide practice questions to challenge future test-takers. *KALLIS' iBT TOEFL® Pattern Series* aims to accomplish all these study tasks by presenting iBT TOEFL® test material in an organized, comprehensive, and easy-to-understand way.

*KALLIS' iBT TOEFL® Pattern Speaking Series* provides in-depth explanations and practices that will help you prepare for the iBT TOEFL speaking section. This study guide focuses on the development of simple, step-by-step response strategies that will guide you when responding to each speaking task.

## Understanding the Speaking Tasks

Chapters 1 through 6 are devoted to explaining and solving each of the six speaking tasks. The beginning of each of these chapters introduces one of the six types of speaking tasks encountered in the iBT TOEFL speaking section. These introductory sections will prepare you for the explanations and practices that follow.

### General Information

The **General Information** section presents the speaking skills that you will need to complete the speaking portion of the iBT TOEFL and provides descriptions of each speaking task.

### Hacking Strategy

The **Hacking Strategy** and corresponding **Example** provide a step-by-step process that explains how to prepare for and respond to each speaking task. While the **Hacking Strategy** develops a common process that can be used to respond to any speaking task, the **Example** demonstrates how this common process can be used to solve one particular type of speaking task.

## Improving Speaking Skills through Practice

A combination of explanations and practices breaks down each speaking task into simple, step-by-step processes.

### Practices

In Chapters 1 through 6, each step of the **Hacking Strategy** is elaborated on with a brief explanation and with one or more **Practices**. These provide opportunities to develop the skills that you just read about. Each **Practice** builds upon information presented earlier in the chapter, allowing you to gradually develop skills that you will use when you are responding to the speaking tasks.

### Exercises

**Exercises** require you to use skills developed in each chapter to complete a speaking task response. Each **Exercise** provides a series of templates that help you organize and compose your response; after each **Exercise**, you will find an Evaluation page that allows you to check the effectiveness of your response. Three **Exercises** are located at the end of each of the task-specific chapters (Chapters 1 through 6).

### Actual Practice

Chapter 7 consists of three **Actual Practices**, which provide templates to help you outline and compose Independent and Integrated speaking responses. Thus, **Actual Practices** require you to use skills from all **Practices**, so **Actual Practices** should be attempted only after you are familiar with the structure of the iBT TOEFL speaking section.

### Actual Test

The **Actual Test** section, which is located in Chapter 8, presents all six speaking tasks in a format that resembles the official iBT TOEFL speaking test. Because this section does not contain the detailed templates given in the **Exercises** or the **Actual Practices**, this section should be attempted only after all speaking skills have been mastered.

## In Case You Need Help

▶ Toward the back of this book, you will find the **Answer Key**, which provides model answers to the **Practices** from Chapters 1 through 6. Additionally, model answers are included immediately after their corresponding **Exercises** and **Actual Practices/Test**.

▶ These model answers demonstrate one acceptable way to answer each question, but there will often be many acceptable answers. So do not feel that your responses must be the same as the model answers, just use them for guidance when necessary.

*Publisher's Note

This first edition of the KALLIS' iBT TOEFL Speaking Series does not yet include audio recordings of the lectures and conversations, as we are setting up our website, which will contain these supplementary materials. Once they are prepared, they will be posted on our website. We apologize for any inconvenicence.

# Table of Contents

## INDEPENDENT SPEAKING

### Chapter 1

**Sharing a Personal Experience**

| | |
|---|---|
| General Background Information | 2 |
| Hacking Strategy | 4 |
| Step 1 | 6 |
| Step 2 | 8 |
| Step 3 | 12 |
| *Exercise 1* | 14 |
| *Exercise 2* | 16 |
| *Exercise 3* | 18 |
| *Model Answer* | 20 |

### Chapter 2

**Selecting a Preference**

| | |
|---|---|
| General Background Information | 24 |
| Hacking Strategy | 26 |
| Step 1 | 28 |
| Step 2 | 30 |
| Step 3 | 34 |
| *Exercise 1* | 36 |
| *Exercise 2* | 38 |
| *Exercise 3* | 40 |
| *Model Answer* | 42 |

## INTEGRATED SPEAKING

### Chapter 3

**Campus Situation** (Reading and Listening)

| | |
|---|---|
| General Background Information | 46 |
| Hacking Strategy | 47 |
| Step 1 | 50 |
| Step 2 | 54 |
| Step 3 | 56 |
| *Exercise 1 & Model Answer* | 58 |
| *Exercise 2 & Model Answer* | 62 |
| *Exercise 3 & Model Answer* | 66 |

### Chapter 4

**Academic Course** (Reading and Listening)

| | |
|---|---|
| General Background Information | 72 |
| Hacking Strategy | 73 |
| Step 1 | 76 |
| Step 2 | 80 |
| Step 3 | 82 |
| *Exercise 1 & Model Answer* | 84 |
| *Exercise 2 & Model Answer* | 88 |
| *Exercise 3 & Model Answer* | 92 |

# SPEAKING 1 FOUNDATION

Ready, set, speak!

## Chapter 5
**Campus Situation** (Listening)
| | |
|---|---|
| General Background Information | 98 |
| Hacking Strategy | 99 |
| Step 1 | 102 |
| Step 2 | 104 |
| Step 3 | 106 |
| | |
| *Exercise 1 & Model Answer* | 108 |
| *Exercise 2 & Model Answer* | 112 |
| *Exercise 3 & Model Answer* | 116 |

## Chapter 6
**Academic Course** (Listening)
| | |
|---|---|
| General Background Information | 122 |
| Hacking Strategy | 123 |
| Step 1 | 126 |
| Step 2 | 128 |
| Step 3 | 130 |
| | |
| *Exercise 1 & Model Answer* | 132 |
| *Exercise 2 & Model Answer* | 136 |
| *Exercise 3 & Model Answer* | 140 |

## Chapter 7
**Actual Practice**
| | |
|---|---|
| Actual Practice 1 | 150 |
| Actual Practice 2 | 166 |
| Actual Practice 3 | 182 |

## Chapter 8
**Actual Test**
| | |
|---|---|
| | 200 |

## Appendix
**Answer Key**
| | |
|---|---|
| | 218 |

# Before You Begin...

## INDEPENDENT AND INTEGRATED TASKS

The iBT TOEFL Speaking test consists of six tasks: two Independent tasks and four Integrated tasks.

The first two tasks are called "Independent tasks" because they require you to produce a response without using any extra written or spoken materials. Thus, you must come up with responses to the first two tasks independently, using your own experiences or opinions.

The last four tasks are called "Integrated tasks" because they require you to incorporate, or integrate, material from spoken and/or written sources into your response. Task 3, for example, will require you to read a passage, listen to a conversation, and then form a response based on what you have read and heard. Two of the Integrated tasks deal with university-related issue, and the other two Integrated tasks discuss academic topics that reflect material that an American-university student might encounter.

## TRANSITION WORDS AND PHRASES

**Transition words and phrases** explain how the content of one sentence relates to the rest of your response.

| Meaning | Examples |
| --- | --- |
| addition | additionally, furthermore, in addition, in fact, moreover |
| cause-and-effect | as a result, consequently, then, therefore, to this end |
| compare/contrast | compared to, despite, however, in contrast, on the contrary, on the one hand, on the other hand, nevertheless |
| conclusions | finally, in conclusion, in summary, lastly, thus, in short |
| examples | for example, for instance, in this case, in this situation |
| introductions | according to, as indicated in/by, based on |
| reasons | one reason is, another reason is, due to |
| sequence | afterward, again, also, and, finally, first, next, previously, second, third |

## SYMBOLS AND ABBREVIATIONS

When taking notes to prepare for a spoken response, save time by using symbols and abbreviations instead of complete words. You can create your own symbols and abbreviations in addition to using those listed in the charts on the following page.

| Symbol | Meaning | Symbol | Meaning |
|---|---|---|---|
| & | and | = | equals, is |
| % | percent | > | more than |
| # | number | < | less than |
| @ | at | → | resulting in |
| ↓ | decreasing | ↑ | increasing |

## ABBREVIATIONS FOR UNIVERSITY ACTIVITIES

| Abbreviation | Meaning | Abbreviation | Meaning |
|---|---|---|---|
| edu. | education | RA | resident assistant |
| GE | general education | stu. | student |
| GPA | grade point average | TA | teaching assistant |
| prof. | professor/professional | univ. | university |

## ABBREVIATIONS FOR ACADEMIC TOPICS

| Abbreviation | Meaning | Abbreviation | Meaning |
|---|---|---|---|
| bio. | biology/biological | exp. | experience/experiment |
| c. | century | info. | information |
| chem. | chemistry/chemical | gov. | government |
| def. | definition | hypo. | hypothesis |
| econ. | economics/economy | phys. | physics/physical |
| env. | environment | psych. | psychology/psychological |
| ex. | example | sci. | science/scientific |

## OTHER ABBREVIATIONS

| Abbreviation | Meaning | Abbreviation | Meaning |
|---|---|---|---|
| abt. | about | pic. | picture |
| b/c | because | ppl. | people |
| comm. | community/communication | pref. | preference |
| e/o | each other | pt. | point |
| fam. | family | ques. | question |
| fav. | favorite | s/b | somebody |
| gen. | general/generation | s/o | someone |
| hr. | hour | sec. | second |
| impt. | important | w/ | with |
| loc. | location | w/i | within |
| lvl. | level | w/o | without |
| min. | minute | yr. | year |

# iBT TOEFL Speaking Task Composition

| Task Type | Task Description | Time (Total 20 Minutes) |
|---|---|---|
| **Independent Tasks** | | |
| 1. Independent Task <Personal Opinion Task> | Speak about your opinion regarding people, places, events, or activities | Preparation Time: 15 Sec<br>Answer Time: 45 Sec |
| 2. Independent Task <Personal Preference Task> | Choose one of two opposing views, and defend your choice | Preparation Time: 15 Sec<br>Answer Time: 45 Sec |
| **Integrated Tasks Read/Listen/Speak** | | |
| 3. Integrated Task <Campus Situation> | *Reading: an announcement regarding a campus-related issue (75-100 words)<br><br>*Listening: a conversation regarding the announcement (60-80 seconds)<br><br>*Responding: summarize the announcement and give the speaker's opinion on the issue | Preparation Time: 30 Sec<br>Answer Time: 60 Sec |
| 4. Integrated Task <Academic Course Topic> | *Reading: terminology or definition of an academic subject (75-100 words)<br><br>*Listening: a lecture giving specific information about the terminology or concept (60-90 seconds)<br><br>*Responding: address the prompt, often by summarizing the reading and the listening | Preparation Time: 30 Sec<br>Answer Time: 60 Sec |
| **Integrated Tasks Listen/Speak** | | |
| 5. Integrated Task <Campus Situation> | *Listening: a conversation that presents a student's and two possible solutions (60-90 minutes)<br><br>*Responding: summarize the problem, state your preferred solution, and support your preference with reasons and details | Preparation Time: 20 Sec<br>Answer Time: 60 Sec |
| 6. Integrated Task <Academic Course Topic> | *Listening: a lecture that explains a term or concept using specific examples. (90-120 minutes)<br><br>*Responding: summarize the lecture and show an understanding of the topic and its details | Preparation Time: 20 Sec<br>Answer Time: 60 Sec |

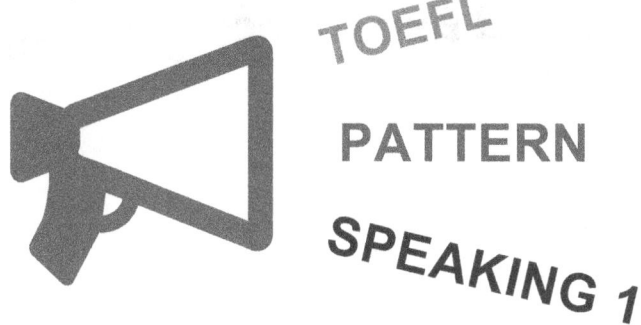

# TOEFL PATTERN SPEAKING 1

## CHAPTER 1

## Sharing a Personal Experience

# Chapter 1: Sharing a Personal Experience

## GENERAL BACKGROUND INFORMATION

### 1. EXPLANATION OF TASK 1

Speaking Task 1 asks you to speak about a personal experience or familiar topic. A narrator will read the prompt aloud; the prompt will stay on the computer screen during your preparation and response times.

You will then have 15 seconds to prepare your response. Begin preparing when the "Preparation Time" notice appears on your screen. Use the time to write down a few notes in outline form because you will not have enough time to write a full answer.

At the end of 15 seconds, you will hear a short beep. The "Preparation Time" notice changes to "Response Time." The countdown from 45 seconds begins. Your response will be recorded during the 45 seconds. At the end, the recording will stop. A new screen will indicate that the response time has ended.

### 2. NECESSARY SKILLS FOR TASK 1

You must be able to:

- recall personal experiences and events and form opinions about them
- organize ideas coherently with a clear topic statement and supporting reasons
- speak clearly using correct grammar, vocabulary, and pronunciation

### 3. EXPLANATION OF QUESTION TYPES

You will see one of two types of questions for the personal experience prompt. In both types of prompt, you must state an opinion and support that opinion with reasons and details.

### Question Types

**1 Describing a Familiar Person, Place, Activity, or Event**

Describe X. Explain how X has affected your life. Use specific reasons and details to support your answer.

**2 Expressing Personal Likes, Dislikes, or Values**

Describe your favorite/least favorite X. Explain why X is your favorite/least favorite. Use specific reasons and examples to support your answer.

## 4. EXAMPLE PROMPTS

Possible Task 1 prompts that you may encounter on the official TOEFL exam include:

> **Prompt**
>
> - Who is the most important person in your life? Use specific reasons and details to support your answer.
>
> - What do you consider your most important achievement? Use specific reasons and details to support your answer.
>
> - Describe the most memorable event or holiday in your life. Use specific reasons and details to support your answer.
>
> - Describe the most important quality of a good teacher. Use specific reasons and details to support your answer.
>
> - Among the cities you have not been to yet, describe the one that you would most like to visit. Use specific reasons and details to support your answer.
>
> - Describe a job that you would like to have. Use specific reasons and details to support your answer.

## 5. USEFUL EXPRESSIONS

Some useful expressions for Task 1 are:

- I think (that) _____.

- I believe (that) _____.

- In my experience, _____.

- The most _____ is _____ because _____.

- The best _____ is _____ because _____.

- The worst _____ is _____ because _____.

- My favorite _____ is _____ because _____.

- My least favorite _____ is _____ because _____.

# HACKING STRATEGY

### STEP 1. OUTLINE YOUR RESPONSE

- Read the prompt carefully
- Decide on an opinion

### STEP 2. PREPARE YOUR RESPONSE

- Make your opinion into a topic statement
- Add reasons that support your opinion

### STEP 3. DELIVER YOUR RESPONSE

- Respond using coherent sentences
- Add transition words between ideas

# EXAMPLE

## STEP 1. OUTLINE YOUR RESPONSE

First, you must read the prompt carefully. Make sure that you understand exactly what the prompt is asking you to do.

> **Prompt**
> Describe your favorite landmark from your hometown. Explain why you enjoy visiting this location. Use specific reasons and details to support your answer.

For this prompt, the first thing that you must decide on is a "favorite landmark from your hometown." Your response to the main part of the prompt is called your *opinion*. After reading the prompt, quickly write down your opinion. Make sure that you choose something that you can talk about for 45 seconds.

- **Opinion:** *fav. landmark → central park in hometown*

## STEP 2. PREPARE YOUR RESPONSE

When organizing your response, you should make your opinion into a topic statement and come up with at least two reasons or details that support your topic statement. Because you are only given 15 seconds to prepare your response, you must organize your thoughts quickly.

- **Topic Statement:** *My favorite landmark in my hometown is its central park.*
  - **Reason 1:** *many museums → learn abt. art, archaeology, plants & sports*
  - **Reason 2:** *nature → many beautiful flowers & trees*

## STEP 3. DELIVER YOUR RESPONSE

Use the outline that you created in STEP 2 to guide you as you deliver your response. Respond using complete sentences, and add transition words to show how ideas relate to one another.

*My favorite landmark in my hometown is its central park. There are two reasons I like visiting this park. **First**, it has many museums that have interesting displays about art, history, archaeology, and sports. **Additionally**, I enjoy walking around the park because it has beautiful scenery with lots of trees, flowers, and plants.*

# STEP 1. OUTLINE YOUR RESPONSE

▶ **APPROACHING A PROMPT**

Make sure that you respond to the entire prompt. One prompt will often ask you to address multiple points.

> **Prompt**
> Name a place that you have enjoyed visiting and would recommend to others. Describe this location and explain why you would recommend it. Use specific reasons and details to support your answer.

This prompt is instructing you to address three related points. You are being asked to:

1) name one place that you enjoyed visiting
2) describe some memorable features of the location
3) explain why others should visit this place

Additionally, the prompt will often tell you to use *specific* reasons, details, and/or examples.

▶ **FORMING AN OPINION**

After reading the prompt, you must form an opinion that addresses the prompt. Because you only have 15 seconds to outline your entire response, coming up with an opinion quickly is crucial.

> **Prompt**
> Name a place that you have enjoyed visiting and would recommend to others. Describe this location and explain why you would recommend it. Use specific reasons and details to support your answer.

Make sure that you choose an opinion that is familiar to you and simple enough to explain in 45 seconds. And remember, you are being scored based on how well you defend your opinion, not based on what particular opinion you select.

Because you should decide on an opinion immediately after reading the prompt, use short phrases to state your opinion.

• Opinion: *enjoyed visiting Mt. Rainier (WA, U.S.)*

**Practice 1** — Below are some broad categories; quickly list two examples for each category. Doing so will help you quickly produce an opinion when answering independent prompts.

1) sports     *football*     *baseball*
2) television shows     _____     _____
3) bands     _____     _____
4) books     _____     _____
5) movies     _____     _____
6) pets     _____     _____
7) types of weather     _____     _____
8) emotions     _____     _____

**Practice 2** — Write down your opinion for each of the prompts below.

1) **Prompt**
What is your most treasured possession?

- Opinion: _____

2) **Prompt**
What is your favorite film genre?

- Opinion: _____

3) **Prompt**
Where do you most enjoy spending your free time?

- Opinion: _____

# STEP 2A. PREPARE YOUR RESPONSE

▶ **FORMING A TOPIC STATEMENT**

The **topic statement** should be the first sentence of your speaking response. It gives your opinion in the form of a statement. Make sure that you choose an opinion that you can support with reasons and details for 45 seconds.

Create a topic statement by including vocabulary from the prompt to provide a clear and concise response to the prompt.

> **Prompt**
> Name a place that you have enjoyed visiting and would recommend to others. Describe this location and explain why you would recommend it. Use specific reasons and details to support your answer.

- **Opinion:** *enjoyed visiting Mt. Rainier (WA, U.S.)*

- **Topic Statement:** *When I visited the U.S., I really enjoyed visiting Mount Rainier National Park in Washington, and I'd recommend this place to others.*

Notice how the topic statement above fully addresses the first point of the prompt by naming one place for a tourist to visit. Moreover, the topic statement above includes information that may be helpful to the listener, such as the name of the state where the national park is located.

**PRACTICE 1** Using the spaces provided below, form an opinion that responds to the prompt, and then rephrase your opinion to form a topic statement.

1)
> **Prompt**
> What is your most treasured possession? Describe the item and explain why it is important to you.

- Opinion: _____

⬇

- Topic Statement: _____
  _____

2)
> **Prompt**
> What is your favorite film genre? Explain why you like this type of movie.

- Opinion: _____

⬇

- Topic Statement: _____
  _____

3)
> **Prompt**
> Where do you most enjoy spending your free time? Describe this location and explain why you enjoy spending time there.

- Opinion: _____

⬇

- Topic Statement: _____
  _____

SHARING A PERSONAL EXPERIENCE ♦ CHAPTER 1

# STEP 2B. PREPARE YOUR RESPONSE

## ADDING REASONS AND DETAILS

Once you have composed a topic statement, you must be able to support your statement using **reasons**. While the topic statement tells the listener what your response to the prompt is, the reasons that you choose tell the listener *why* you have chosen this particular topic statement.

When preparing your response, do not use full sentences to write down your reasons; just write down essential information that you can turn into a full response later.

> **Prompt**
> Name a place that you have enjoyed visiting and would recommend to others. Describe this location and explain why you would recommend it. Use specific reasons and details to support your answer.

- **Topic Statement:** *When I visited the U.S., I really enjoyed visiting Mount Rainier National Park in Washington, and I'd recommend this place to others.*

During your preparation time, write down the key points that you can expand upon in your response.

- **Notes**
    - **Reason 1:** *beautiful scenery → forests, mountains, active volcano*
    - **Reason 2:** *great hiking; saw wildlife*

Make sure that the reasons you come up with relate to your topic statement. Getting off-topic in your response will make your response less coherent and lower your score.

**PRACTICE 1** Using your topic statement from the previous exercise, write down two reasons that support your topic statement in a brief note format.

1)
> **Prompt**
> What is your most treasured possession? Describe the item and explain why it is important to you. Use specific reasons and details in your response.

- Topic Statement: _____

▶ Notes
- Reason 1: _____
- Reason 2: _____

2)
> **Prompt**
> What is your favorite film genre? Explain why you like this type of movie. Use specific reasons and details in your response.

- Topic Statement: _____

▶ Notes
- Reason 1: _____
- Reason 2: _____

3)
> **Prompt**
> Where do you most enjoy spending your free time? Describe this location and explain why you enjoy spending time there. Support your response with specific reasons and details.

- Topic Statement: _____

▶ Notes
- Reason 1: _____
- Reason 2: _____

# STEP 3. DELIVER YOUR RESPONSE

Now you have all the pieces of information that you need to deliver your response.

> **Prompt**
> Name a place that you have enjoyed visiting and would recommend to others. Describe this location and explain why you would recommend it. Use specific reasons and details to support your answer.

- The first sentence of your response should present your opinion in the form of a **topic statement**.

- Give **two reasons** that support your topic statement. Use any notes that you have for guidance, but make sure that you respond using complete sentences.

- When you respond, include **transition words** where they are appropriate. Doing so will clarify the relationships between ideas. See below for a sample of a completed response.

**Example Response**

| | Notes | Response |
|---|---|---|
| **Topic Statement** | enjoyed visiting Mt. Rainier (WA, U.S.) | When I visited the U.S., I really enjoyed visiting Mount Rainier National Park in Washington, and I'd recommend this place to others. |
| **Reasons** | beautiful scenery; forests, mountains, active volcano | **For one**, Mount Rainier contains beautiful scenery. I was able to see massive forests, snow-capped mountains, and an active volcano. |
| | great hiking; saw wildlife | **Additionally**, the national park has incredible hiking trails. Many of the trails were challenging, but I was rewarded with many wildlife sightings, such as deer walking near the trail. |

Following the steps below, develop a Task 1 response to the following prompt.

1)
> **Prompt**
> Describe a holiday or tradition that is unique to your country. Explain what makes this holiday or tradition special. Use reasons and details to support your answer.

- Opinion: _____

- Topic Statement: _____
  _____

  - Reason 1: _____
  - Reason 2: _____

Now that you have created an outline, write down a full-length response. Once you have written down your response, **say it aloud to yourself, a friend, a classmate, or a family member**.

**Response**

_____
_____
_____
_____
_____
_____
_____
_____
_____
_____

# EXERCISE 1

Following the steps below, develop a response to the following prompt.

## STEP 1. OUTLINE YOUR RESPONSE

**Prompt**
Describe your favorite teacher. Explain why this teacher is your favorite. Use specific reasons and details to support your answer.

- Opinion: _____

## STEP 2. PREPARE YOUR RESPONSE    00:00:15

- Topic Statement: My favorite teacher is _____.
  - Reason 1: _____
  - Reason 2: _____

## STEP 3. DELIVER YOUR RESPONSE    00:00:45

### Response

My favorite teacher is _____. The first characteristic I like about _____ is _____
_____.

Another characteristic I like about _____ is _____
_____
_____.

# Evaluation

**Now practice saying your response aloud.** If possible, have a friend or a classmate fill out this checklist as you say your response to him or her. If you are by yourself, record and listen to your response, and then fill out the checklist below on your own.

Deliver your response within 45 seconds.

## Task 1 Response Checklist

|  | Yes | Somewhat | No |
|---|---|---|---|
| • Does the speaker give his or her opinion in a topic statement? |  |  |  |
| • Does the speaker support his or her opinion with at least two details or reasons? |  |  |  |
| • Does the speaker deliver an organized response by using transition words and proper sentence structures? |  |  |  |
| • Does the speaker deliver a coherent response by using appropriate tone and pronunciation? |  |  |  |
| • Does the speaker finish within the time limit? |  |  | ✗ |

# EXERCISE 2

Following the steps below, develop a response to the following prompt.

## STEP 1. OUTLINE YOUR RESPONSE

**Prompt**
What is your favorite type of music? Describe the genre and explain why you enjoy this type of music. Use specific reasons and details to support your answer.

- Opinion: _____

## STEP 2. PREPARE YOUR RESPONSE                    00:00:15

- Topic Statement: My favorite type of music is _____.
  - Reason 1: _____
  - Reason 2: _____

## STEP 3. DELIVER YOUR RESPONSE                    00:00:45

**Response**

My favorite type of music is _____. One characteristic I like about _____ _____ is _____
_____.
Another characteristic I like about _____ is _____
_____
_____.

*Evaluation*

**Now practice saying your response aloud.** If possible, have a friend or a classmate fill out this checklist as you say your response to him or her. If you are by yourself, record and listen to your response, and then fill out the checklist below on your own.

Deliver your response within 45 seconds.

## Task 1 Response Checklist

|  | Yes | Somewhat | No |
|---|---|---|---|
| • Does the speaker give his or her opinion in a topic statement? | | | |
| • Does the speaker support his or her opinion with at least two details or reasons? | | | |
| • Does the speaker deliver an organized response by using transition words and proper sentence structures? | | | |
| • Does the speaker deliver a coherent response by using appropriate tone and pronunciation? | | | |
| • Does the speaker finish within the time limit? | | ✗ | |

# EXERCISE 3

Following the steps below, develop a response to the following prompt.

## STEP 1. OUTLINE YOUR RESPONSE

**Prompt**
What is your least favorite subject in school? Explain why you do not enjoy this subject. Use specific reasons and details to support your answer.

- Opinion: _____

## STEP 2. PREPARE YOUR RESPONSE       00:00:15

- Topic Statement: My least favorite subject is _____.
    - Reason 1: _____
    - Reason 2: _____

## STEP 3. DELIVER YOUR RESPONSE       00:00:45

**Response**

My least favorite subject in school is _____. The first reason I dislike this subject is _____

_____.

Another reason I dislike this subject is _____

_____

_____.

# Evaluation

**Now practice saying your response aloud.** If possible, have a friend or a classmate fill out this checklist as you say your response to him or her. If you are by yourself, record and listen to your response, and then fill out the checklist below on your own.

Deliver your response within 45 seconds.

## Task 1 Response Checklist

|  | Yes | Somewhat | No |
|---|---|---|---|
| • Does the speaker give his or her opinion in a topic statement? | | | |
| • Does the speaker support his or her opinion with at least two details or reasons? | | | |
| • Does the speaker deliver an organized response by using transition words and proper sentence structures? | | | |
| • Does the speaker deliver a coherent response by using appropriate tone and pronunciation? | | | |
| • Does the speaker finish within the time limit? | | | ✗ |

# MODEL ANSWER

## EXERCISE 1

### STEP 1. OUTLINE YOUR RESPONSE

**Prompt**

Describe your favorite teacher. Explain why this teacher is your favorite. Use specific reasons and details to support your answer.

- Opinion: *fav. teacher = Ms. Richards, high school English*

### STEP 2. PREPARE YOUR RESPONSE

- Topic Statement: *My favorite teacher is my high school English teacher, Ms. Richards.*
  - Reason 1: *taught me how to write well, clearly*
  - Reason 2: *encouraged me to pursue writing*

### STEP 3. DELIVER YOUR RESPONSE

My favorite teacher is my high school English teacher, Ms. Richards. The first characteristic I like about Ms. Richards is her incredible knowledge of the English language. She taught me almost everything I know about writing. **For example**, she showed me how to form a thesis and how to outline before writing an essay. Another characteristic I like about Ms. Richards is her positive, encouraging personality. Whether my essays were good or bad, she always gave great feedback. **Moreover**, she encouraged me to pursue writing outside of school, which has inspired me to major in creative writing once I get accepted into a university.

## EXERCISE 2

### STEP 1. OUTLINE YOUR RESPONSE

**Prompt**

What is your favorite type of music? Describe the genre and explain why you enjoy this type of music. Use specific reasons and details to support your answer.

- Opinion: *fav. music = classical music*

### STEP 2. PREPARE YOUR RESPONSE

- Topic Statement: *My favorite type of music is classical music.*
  - Reason 1: *often relaxing, good for studying b/c no words (Mozart)*
  - Reason 2: *can be exciting, expresses emotion (Beethoven)*

### STEP 3. DELIVER YOUR RESPONSE

*My favorite type of music is classical music. One characteristic I like about classical music is that it's often relaxing, which makes it perfect to listen to while studying.* **For instance**, *I enjoy listening to Mozart's piano concertos when preparing for a test. The soothing piano calms me, but the complexity of the music keeps my mind working. Another characteristic I like about classical music is that some of it can be quite exciting. Often, when I'm driving or exercising, I enjoy listening to Beethoven's symphonies. These works express a huge range of emotions and make me feel like I can overcome any obstacle.*

## EXERCISE 3

### STEP 1. OUTLINE YOUR RESPONSE

> **Prompt**
> What is your least favorite subject in school? Explain why you do not enjoy this subject. Use specific reasons and details to support your answer.

- Opinion: *least fav. subject = math*

### STEP 2. PREPARE YOUR RESPONSE

- Topic Statement: *My least favorite subject is mathematics.*
  - Reason 1: *doesn't seem very useful*
  - Reason 2: *too many abstract formulas to memorize*

### STEP 3. DELIVER YOUR RESPONSE

*My least favorite subject in school is mathematics. The first reason I dislike this subject is because I can rarely find a practical application for subjects like algebra and calculus in my daily life.* **For example**, *I spent a lot of time learning about derivatives in calculus, but I've never needed to use them in my daily life. Another reason I dislike this subject is because I have difficulty memorizing the formulas used in higher math. I often get one part of a formula mixed up with another, which causes me to mess up entire problems.*

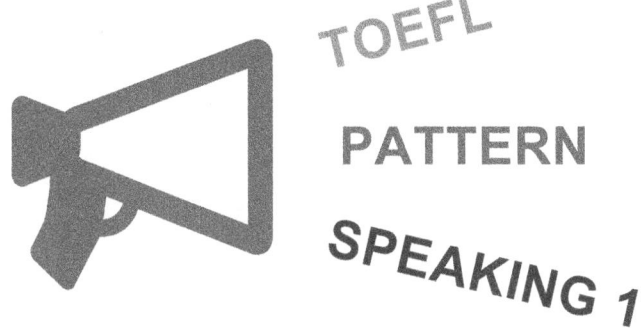

# CHAPTER 2
## Selecting a Preference

# Chapter 2: Selecting a Preference

## GENERAL BACKGROUND INFORMATION

### 1. EXPLANATION OF TASK 2

Speaking Task 2 presents two possible activities, situations, or opinions. Choose which one of the two options you prefer, and then explain your preference with reasons and details. A narrator will read the prompt aloud; the prompt will stay on the computer screen during your preparation and response time.

You will then have 15 seconds to prepare your response. Begin preparing when the "Preparation Time" notice appears on your screen. Use the time to write down a few notes in outline form because you will not have enough time to write a full answer.

At the end of 15 seconds, you will hear a short beep. The "Preparation Time" notice changes to "Response Time." The countdown from 45 seconds begins. Your response will be recorded during the 45 seconds. At the end, the recording will stop. A new screen will indicate that the response time has ended.

### 2. NECESSARY SKILLS FOR TASK 2

You must be able to:

- take a position and support the position with reasons
- organize ideas coherently with a clear topic statement and supporting reasons
- speak clearly using correct grammar, vocabulary, and pronunciation

### 3. EXPLANATION OF QUESTION TYPES

The question will always ask that you respond with your preference and give reasons for your response. Your score is not based upon your preference but on how well you explain your preference.

### Question Types

**1  Picking a Preference about a University Issue**

Some students prefer X (first university-related preference). Other students prefer Y (second university-related preference). Which do you prefer and why? Use specific reasons and examples to support your answer.

**2  Picking a Lifestyle or Ethical Preference**

Some people believe X (first lifestyle/ethical preference). Other people believe Y (second lifestyle/ethical preference). Which opinion do you agree with and why? Use specific details and examples to support your preference.

## 4. EXAMPLE PROMPTS

Possible Task 2 prompts that you may encounter on the official TOEFL exam include:

> **Prompt**
>
> - Do you agree or disagree with the following statement? People do not communicate effectively anymore because of distracting technological developments such as cable television and the Internet. Use specific reasons and details to support your answer.
>
> - Some people make decisions quickly. Others only make decisions after thinking about their choice for a long time. Which approach do you prefer and why? Use specific reasons and details to support your answer.
>
> - Some students prefer choosing their own roommates while others prefer having the university choose their roommates for them. Which do you prefer and why? Use specific reasons and details to support your answer.
>
> - Do you agree or disagree with the following statement? Advertisements have too much influence on people's decision. Use specific reasons and details to support your answer.
>
> - Some people believe that a college or university education should be available to all students. Others believe that higher education should be available only to students who perform well academically. Which view do you agree with and why? Use specific reasons and details to support your answer.

## 5. USEFUL EXPRESSIONS

Some useful expressions for Task 2 are:

- In my opinion, _____.

- I agree (that) _____ because _____.

- I disagree (that) _____ because _____.

- I prefer _____ to _____ because _____.
  (noun / noun phrase) (noun / noun phrase)

- I prefer to _____ than to _____ because _____.
  (verb / verb phrase) (verb / verb phrase)

- I think (that) _____ is better than _____ because _____.

- I believe (that) _____ is preferable to _____ because _____.

- Given the choice between _____ and _____, I prefer _____ because _____.

# HACKING STRATEGY

### STEP 1. OUTLINE YOUR RESPONSE

- Read the prompt carefully
- Decide on a preference

### STEP 2. PREPARE YOUR RESPONSE

- Make your opinion into a topic statement
- Add reasons that support your preference

### STEP 3. DELIVER YOUR RESPONSE

- Respond using coherent sentences
- Add transition words between ideas

# EXAMPLE

## STEP 1. OUTLINE YOUR RESPONSE

First, you must read the prompt carefully. Make sure that you understand exactly what the prompt is asking you to do.

> **Prompt**
> Some students prefer group projects while others prefer working on their own. Which method do you prefer and why? Use specific reasons and examples to support your answer.

For this prompt, the first thing that you must decide on is whether you prefer to work on projects with others or by yourself. Your response to the main part of the prompt is called your *preference*. After reading the prompt, quickly write down your preference. Make sure that you choose something that you can talk about for 45 seconds.

- Preference: *working on my own*

## STEP 2. PREPARE YOUR RESPONSE

When organizing your response, you should make your preference into a topic statement and come up with at least two reasons or details that support your topic statement. Because you are only given 15 seconds to prepare your response, you must organize your thoughts quickly.

- Topic Statement: *I prefer to work on projects on my own for several reasons.*
   - Reason 1: *learn more about the subject*
   - Reason 2: *more control over outcome*

## STEP 3. DELIVER YOUR RESPONSE

Use the outline that you created in STEP 2 to guide you as you deliver your response. Respond using complete sentences, and add transition words to show how ideas relate to one another.

*I prefer to work on projects on my own for several reasons.* **First**, *I enjoy working on my own because when I work alone, I get to learn more about the subject than if I worked in a group.* **Moreover**, *I find working alone beneficial because I have complete control over the outcome of the project.*

# STEP 1. OUTLINE YOUR RESPONSE

▶ **APPROACHING A PROMPT**

Make sure that you respond to the entire prompt. One prompt will often ask you to address multiple points.

> **Prompt**
> Some people like to eat at restaurants. Others like to eat at home. Which do you prefer and why? Support your answer with reasons.

This prompt is instructing you to address two related points. You are being asked to:

1) identify your preferred dining location
2) state why you have this preference

Additionally, the prompt will always tell you to use *specific* reasons, details, and/or examples.

▶ **SELECTING A PREFERENCE**

All Task 2 prompts ask you to select one of two options. Because you only have 15 seconds to outline your entire response, deciding upon a preference quickly is crucial.

> **Prompt**
> Some people like to eat at restaurants. Others like to eat at home. Which do you prefer and why? Support your answer with reasons.

Make sure that you select the option that you feel comfortable talking about for 45 seconds. And remember, you are being scored based on how well you defend your preference, not based on which particular preference you select.

Because you should decide on your preference immediately after reading the prompt, use short phrases to state your preference.

- Preference: *dining @ restaurants*

**PRACTICE 1** Below are some opposing viewpoints. Quickly choose which view you agree with and write down your response.

1) living alone vs. living with roommates

   *I prefer living alone to living with roommates.*

2) having one career during a lifetime vs. having more than one career

   _____

3) living in a small town vs. living in a large city

   _____

4) going to college right after school vs. taking a break for a year

   _____

5) choosing work you love that pays poorly vs. choosing work you do not love that pays well

   _____

**PRACTICE 2** Write down your preference for each of the prompts below.

1) **Prompt**
   Do you prefer writing an essay by hand or by typing it on the computer?

   • Preference: _____

2) **Prompt**
   In their daily lives, some people like following a schedule, while others prefer to be spontaneous and not follow a schedule. Which do you prefer?

   • Preference: _____

3) **Prompt**
   Some people enjoy studying mathematics and the sciences. Others enjoy learning about the humanities (history, art, etc.). Which of these subjects do you prefer to study?

   • Preference: _____

# STEP 2A. PREPARE YOUR RESPONSE

▶ **FORMING A TOPIC STATEMENT**

The **topic statement** should be the first sentence of your speaking response. It gives your preference in the form of a statement. Make sure that you choose a preference that you can support with reasons and details for 45 seconds.

Create a topic statement by including vocabulary from the prompt to provide a clear and concise response to the prompt.

> **Prompt**
> Some people like to eat at restaurants. Others like to eat at home. Which do you prefer? Support your answer with reasons.

- Preference: *dining @ restaurants*

- Topic Statement: *Some people like to eat at home, but I prefer to eat at restaurants.*

Notice how the topic statement above fully addresses the prompt by presenting a preferred dining location.

**PRACTICE 1** Using the spaces provided below, form a preference that responds to the prompt; then rephrase your preference into a topic statement.

1)
> **Prompt**
> Do you prefer writing an essay by hand or by typing it on the computer? Explain your preference using reasons and details.

- Preference: _____

- Topic Statement: _____
_____

2)
> **Prompt**
> In their daily lives, some people like following a schedule, while others prefer to be spontaneous and not follow a schedule. Which do you prefer? Explain your preference.

- Preference: _____

- Topic Statement: _____
_____

3)
> **Prompt**
> Some people enjoy studying mathematics and the sciences. Others enjoy learning about the humanities (history, art, etc.). Which of these subjects do you prefer to study? Explain your preference.

- Preference: _____

- Topic Statement: _____
_____

SELECTING A PREFERENCE ♦ CHAPTER 2

# STEP 2B. PREPARE YOUR RESPONSE

▶ **ADDING REASONS AND DETAILS**

Once you have composed a topic statement, you must be able to support your statement using **reasons.** While the topic statement tells the listener what your response to the prompt is, the reasons that you choose tell the listener why you have chosen this particular topic statement.

When preparing your response, do not use full sentences to write down your reasons; just write down essential information that you can turn into a full response later.

> **Prompt**
> Some people like to eat at restaurants. Others like to eat at home. Which do you prefer? Support your answer with reasons.

- Topic Statement: *Some people like to eat at home, but I prefer to eat at restaurants.*

During your preparation time, write down the key points that you can expand upon in your response.

▶ Notes
- Reason 1: *relaxing after busy day*
- Reason 2: *offers variety*

Make sure that the reasons you come up with relate to your topic sentence. Getting off-topic in your response will make your response less coherent and lower your score.

 **Practice 1** Using your topic statement from the previous exercise, write down two reasons that support your topic statement in a brief note format.

1)
**Prompt**
Do you prefer writing an essay by hand or by typing it on the computer? Explain your preference using reasons and details.

- Topic Statement: _____
_____

▶ Notes
- Reason 1: _____
- Reason 2: _____

2)
**Prompt**
In their daily lives, some people like following a schedule, while others prefer to be spontaneous and not follow a schedule. Which do you prefer? Explain your preference.

- Topic Statement: _____
_____

▶ Notes
- Reason 1: _____
- Reason 2: _____

3)
**Prompt**
Some people enjoy studying mathematics and the sciences. Others enjoy learning about the humanities (history, art, etc.). Which of these subjects do you prefer to study? Explain your preference.

- Topic Statement: _____
_____

▶ Notes
- Reason 1: _____
- Reason 2: _____

# STEP 3. DELIVER YOUR RESPONSE

Now you have all the pieces of information that you need to deliver your response.

> **Prompt**
> Some people like to eat at restaurants. Others like to eat at home. Which do you prefer? Support your answer with reasons.

- The first sentence of your response should present your preference in the form of a **topic statement**.

- Then give the **two reasons** that support your topic statement. Use any notes that you have for guidance, but make sure that you respond in complete sentences.

- When you respond, include **transition words** where they are appropriate. Doing so will clarify the relationships between ideas. See below for a sample of a completed response.

### Example Response

|  | Notes | Response |
|---|---|---|
| **Topic Statement** | dining @ restaurants | Some people like to eat at home, but I prefer to eat at restaurants. |
| **Reasons** | relaxing after busy day | **First**, eating at restaurants is pleasant because the staff prepares my food as I relax after my busy day. |
|  | offers variety | **Moreover**, dining at restaurants offers more variety. I can taste many different types of food by eating at different restaurants. |

**Practice 1** Following the steps below, develop a Task 2 response to the following prompt.

1)
**Prompt**
Some university students ask their professors for help with challenging tasks or confusing topics. Other students prefer receiving help from their friends or peers. Which option do you prefer? Explain your preference using reasons and details.

- Preference: _____

- Topic Statement: _____
  _____

  - Reason 1: _____
  - Reason 2: _____

Now that you have created an outline, write down a full-length response. Once you have written down your response, **say it aloud to yourself, a friend, a classmate, or a family member**.

**Response**

_____
_____
_____
_____
_____
_____
_____
_____
_____
_____
_____

# EXERCISE 1

Following the steps below, develop a response to the following prompt.

## STEP 1. OUTLINE YOUR RESPONSE

**Prompt**
Some students prefer studying early in the morning while others prefer studying at night. Which study method do you prefer? Use specific reasons and examples to support your answer.

- Preference: _____

## STEP 2. PREPARE YOUR RESPONSE

00:00:15

- Topic Statement: Personally, I prefer studying (**in the morning / at night**).
    - Reason 1: _____
    - Reason 2: _____

## STEP 3. DELIVER YOUR RESPONSE

00:00:45

**Response**

Personally, I prefer studying (**in the morning / at night**). One reason I choose to study at this time is _____

_____.

(**Moreover / However**), I find studying at this time beneficial because _____

_____

_____.

# Evaluation

**Now practice saying your response aloud.** If possible, have a friend/classmate fill out this checklist as you say your response to him or her. If you are by yourself, record and listen to your response, and then fill out the checklist below on your own.

Deliver your response within 45 seconds.

## Task 2 Response Checklist

|   | Yes | Somewhat | No |
|---|---|---|---|
| • Does the speaker give his or her preference in a topic statement? | | | |
| • Does the speaker support his or her preference with at least two details or reasons? | | | |
| • Does the speaker deliver an organized response by using transition words and proper sentence structures? | | | |
| • Does the speaker deliver a coherent response by using appropriate tone and pronunciation? | | | |
| • Does the speaker finish within the time limit? | | ✗ | |

# EXERCISE 2

Following the steps below, develop a response to the following prompt.

## STEP 1. OUTLINE YOUR RESPONSE

**Prompt**
Do you prefer studying with friends or studying by yourself? Explain your preference using reasons and details.

- Preference: _____

## STEP 2. PREPARE YOUR RESPONSE

00:00:15

- Topic Statement: Generally, I prefer studying (**by myself / with friends**).
    - Reason 1: _____
    - Reason 2: _____

## STEP 3. DELIVER YOUR RESPONSE

00:00:45

### Response

Generally, I prefer studying (**by myself / with friends**). The first reason I prefer studying (**by myself / with friends**) is _____

_____.

(**Moreover / However**), I prefer studying (**by myself / with friends**) because _____

_____

_____.

# Evaluation

**Now practice saying your response aloud.** If possible, have a friend/classmate fill out this checklist as you say your response to him or her. If you are by yourself, record and listen to your response, and then fill out the checklist below on your own.

Deliver your response within 45 seconds.

## Task 2 Response Checklist

|  | Yes | Somewhat | No |
|---|---|---|---|
| • Does the speaker give his or her preference in a topic statement? | | | |
| • Does the speaker support his or her preference with at least two details or reasons? | | | |
| • Does the speaker deliver an organized response by using transition words and proper sentence structures? | | | |
| • Does the speaker deliver a coherent response by using appropriate tone and pronunciation? | | | |
| • Does the speaker finish within the time limit? | | | ✗ |

# EXERCISE 3

Following the steps below, develop a response to the following prompt.

## STEP 1. OUTLINE YOUR RESPONSE

**Prompt**
Which do you prefer: living with a roommate or having a room to yourself? Explain your preference using specific reasons and details.

- Preference: _____

## STEP 2. PREPARE YOUR RESPONSE

00:00:15

- Topic Statement: I would rather live (**with a roommate / by myself**).
    - Reason 1: _____
    - Reason 2: _____

## STEP 3. DELIVER YOUR RESPONSE

00:00:45

### 🔊 Response

If I had to choose between the two living situations, I'd rather live (**with a roommate / by myself**). One reason is that _____
_____.

(**Moreover / However**), I prefer living (**with a roommate / by myself**) because _____
_____
_____

# Evaluation

**Now practice saying your response aloud.** If possible, have a friend/classmate fill out this checklist as you say your response to him or her. If you are by yourself, record and listen to your response, and then fill out the checklist below on your own.

Deliver your response within 45 seconds.

## Task 2 Response Checklist

|  | Yes | Somewhat | No |
|---|---|---|---|
| • Does the speaker give his or her preference in a topic statement? | | | |
| • Does the speaker support his or her preference with at least two details or reasons? | | | |
| • Does the speaker deliver an organized response by using transition words and proper sentence structures? | | | |
| • Does the speaker deliver a coherent response by using appropriate tone and pronunciation? | | | |
| • Does the speaker finish within the time limit? | | ✗ | |

# MODEL ANSWER

## EXERCISE 1

### STEP 1. OUTLINE YOUR RESPONSE

**Prompt**

Some students prefer studying early in the morning while others prefer studying at night. Which study method do you prefer? Use specific reasons and examples to support your answer.

- Preference: *study @ night*

### STEP 2. PREPARE YOUR RESPONSE

- Topic Statement: *I prefer studying at night.*
    - Reason 1: *less busy at night, less distraction → more focus*
    - Reason 2: *better time for study groups*

### STEP 3. DELIVER YOUR RESPONSE

*Personally, I prefer studying at night. One reason I choose to study at this time is that I'm less busy in the evening than I am during the morning. Because I have fewer things to do at night, I can focus all my attention on finishing my studies.* **Moreover**, *I find studying at this time beneficial because some of my friends are also available in the evening.* **Thus**, *my friends and I often meet at a coffee shop to study together. These study sessions are usually both fun and productive.*

## EXERCISE 2

### STEP 1. OUTLINE YOUR RESPONSE

**Prompt**

Do you prefer studying with friends or studying by yourself? Explain your preference using reasons and details.

- Preference: *studying by myself*

### STEP 2. PREPARE YOUR RESPONSE

- Topic Statement: *I prefer studying by myself.*
    - Reason 1: *easily distracted, can't multitask*
    - Reason 2: *few friends → same schedule as me*

### STEP 3. DELIVER YOUR RESPONSE

*Generally, I prefer studying by myself. The first reason I prefer studying by myself is that I'm easily distracted, so I'm usually unproductive when I study in groups. Whenever I study in a group, I end up doing more socializing than studying. **Therefore**, it's in my best interest to study alone. **Moreover**, I prefer studying by myself because my friends and I have completely different schedules. Whenever I try to set up a study group, everyone cancels because of scheduling conflicts. **Hence**, it's much more practical for me to study alone.*

## EXERCISE 3

### STEP 1. OUTLINE YOUR RESPONSE

> **Prompt**
> Which do you prefer: living with a roommate or having a room to yourself? Explain your preference using specific reasons and details.

- Preference: *having a room to myself*

### STEP 2. PREPARE YOUR RESPONSE

- Topic Statement: *I'd rather live by myself.*
  - Reason 1: *no siblings, grew up w/ privacy*
  - Reason 2: *can have friends come to visit if lonely*

### STEP 3. DELIVER YOUR RESPONSE

*If I had to choose between the two living situations, I'd rather live by myself. One reason is that I grew up without siblings, so I've never had to share a room before. **As a result**, I enjoy having privacy, so I prefer to live by myself. **Moreover**, I prefer living by myself because I can always meet up with my friends or have them come visit me if I feel lonely. I like being able to control when I have time to myself, so living alone is definitely the best living situation for me.*

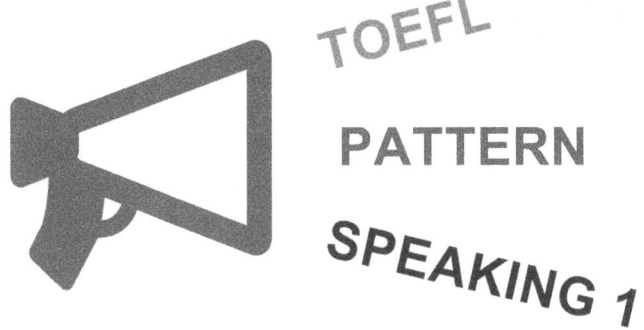

# CHAPTER 3

# Campus Situation
(Reading and Listening)

# Chapter 3 Campus Situation

## GENERAL BACKGROUND INFORMATION

### 1. EXPLANATION OF TASK 3

Speaking Task 3 requires that you read a brief announcement of 75 to 100 words about a change on campus; the announcement may be presented in the form of a newspaper article or a campus-wide notification. You will be given 45 to 50 seconds to read the announcement. Common topics include:

- building, updating, or improving structures on campus
- creating and enforcing new campus rules and regulations
- changing admission, registration, or graduation requirements

The announcement presents information about a proposed change to campus, including two or more reasons for this change.

After reading the announcement, you will listen to two students discuss the subject presented in the announcement. One speaker will either strongly support or oppose the change. The conversation is 60 to 80 seconds long.

After the conversation ends, you will be given a prompt related to what you have read and heard. The prompt appears on your computer screen and is read aloud by a narrator.

> **Prompt**
> The man/woman expresses his/her opinion about the plan described in the announcement. Briefly summarize the plan. Then state his/her opinion about the plan and explain the reasons he/she gives for holding that opinion.

After seeing the prompt, you have 30 seconds of "Preparation Time" to prepare your response. At the end, you will hear a short beep. The clock then changes to "Response Time" and begins to count down.

You have 60 seconds to respond. At the end of the 60 seconds, the recording ends and a new message alerts you that the response time is over.

You may take notes while reading, listening, and preparing. You also may check your notes when responding to the question.

### 2. NECESSARY SKILLS FOR TASK 3

You must be able to:

- understand information from written and spoken sources regarding campus-based subject matter
- identify and summarize major points and important details from written and spoken sources
- synthesize information from written and spoken sources

# HACKING STRATEGY

### STEP 1. OUTLINE YOUR RESPONSE

- Take notes as you read the announcement
- Take notes as you listen to the conversation
- Read the prompt carefully

### STEP 2. PREPARE YOUR RESPONSE

- Summarize the university's announcement
- State the student's opinion regarding the announcement
- State the student's reasons for holding this opinion

### STEP 3. DELIVER YOUR RESPONSE

- Respond using coherent sentences
- Add transition words between ideas

# HACKING STRATEGY EXAMPLE

## STEP 1. OUTLINE YOUR RESPONSE

Take notes on essential information as you read the university's announcement and listen to the conversation. Do not take notes using full sentences, as you will not have time to do so.

### UNIVERSITY ANNOUNCEMENT

**University to Cut Classes**

Because of severe budget cuts, the university must discontinue several classes next year. The administration has decided to cut Italian and Portuguese language classes, as well as some introductory music classes. Hopefully, these cuts will prevent any tuition increases in the coming years.

### CONVERSATION

**M:** I can't believe they're cutting so many great classes!

**F:** Yeah, but the proposal says it's for a good cause.

**M:** Instead of eliminating classes, they should stop building the new football stadium. But we all know that won't happen because football makes the school money while language and music classes don't.

**F:** I guess that's true.

**M:** And keeping a handful of classes would only require a tiny tuition increase. Cutting these interesting classes will make our university less unique; we need to keep these classes!

**F:** You know what, you're right. We should really do something about this!

**M:** Male Student / **F:** Female Student

### ANNOUNCEMENT NOTES

**Proposal:** *cut some lang./music classes*

- **Reason 1:** *severe budget cuts*
- **Reason 2:** *avoid raising student tuition*

### CONVERSATION NOTES

**Speaker's opinion:** *man opposes*

- **Reason 1:** *stop stadium construction, not cut classes*
- **Reason 2:** *keeping classes → little $; classes make univ. interesting*

Once you have taken notes on the announcement and the conversation, carefully read the prompt.

> **Prompt**
>
> The man expresses his opinion regarding the university's announcement. State his opinion and explain the reasons he gives for holding this opinion.

## STEP 2. PREPARE YOUR RESPONSE

During the 30-second preparation time, make sure that your notes address all the points in the prompt, and use the information in your notes to organize your response. Because you only have 30 seconds to prepare your response, do not write using complete sentences.

1) Make sure that you can summarize the proposal in the university's announcement.
    **From Notes** → Proposal: *cut some language/music classes*

2) Make sure that you know whether the speaker supports or opposes the proposal.
    **From Notes** → Speaker's opinion: *man opposes*

3) Make sure that you know why the student either supports or opposes the proposal.
    **From Notes** → Reason 1: *stop stadium construction, not cut classes*
    → Reason 2: *keeping classes → little money; classes make university interesting*

## STEP 3. DELIVER YOUR RESPONSE

Use the outline that you created in STEP 2 to guide you as you deliver your response. Respond using complete sentences, and add transition words to show how ideas relate to one another.

*The university will cut some language and music classes due to major budget cuts. The man states that he opposes getting rid of these classes. The man thinks the university should stop the construction of the new football stadium as an alternative way to save money. **Additionally**, he feels that keeping the language classes is worth a small increase in tuition because these classes make the university unique.*

# STEP 1A. OUTLINE YOUR RESPONSE

## NOTE-TAKING STRATEGIES

Taking notes quickly during the reading and listening portions of this task is crucial, as you can use your notes to help outline your speaking response. When taking notes, you should be able to **abbreviate**, or shorten, common words or phrases and **condense information** in order to save time.

**Tips for taking notes**

- Only write down key points/information that you will use in your response.
- Because of time constraints, do not write using full sentences.
- Make sure that you can understand your own abbreviations.

## TAKING NOTES ON THE UNIVERSITY ANNOUNCEMENT

The passage will present a university-related announcement along with one or more reasons justifying the announcement. Therefore, successful notes will summarize the announcement and list the reasons for the change.

---

**UNIVERSITY ANNOUNCEMENT**

### Tuition Increase

The university must raise tuition next year. For five years, tuition has stayed the same. However, now we have more students. We need more professors and classrooms. We also must improve some of our facilities, which includes upgrading our laboratory equipment and computer labs.

**ANNOUNCEMENT NOTES**

Proposal: ↑ *tuition next yr.*

- Reason 1: *need more prof. & classroom*
- Reason 2: *upgrade facilities*

 **Practice 1** Read the university's announcement and fill out the note template that follows.

### UNIVERSITY ANNOUNCEMENT

**New Parking Lot**

The university proposes to build a new parking lot next year. There are nearly 2,000 more students here now than there were five years ago. The current parking areas cannot provide the spaces needed for the increase. The parking lot will be built over a grassy field near the center of campus, which will save students and instructors time when they walk from the parking lot to class. To pay for the parking lot, the university will increase each student's tuition by $100.

### ANNOUNCEMENT NOTES

Proposal: _____

- Reason 1: _____

  _____

- Reason 2: _____

  _____

CAMPUS SITUATION ♦ CHAPTER 3

# STEP 1B. OUTLINE YOUR RESPONSE

## ▶ TAKING NOTES ON THE CONVERSATION

The conversation will present one speaker who either supports or opposes the university's announcement. In your notes, you should identify the speaker's opinion and list the reasons that the speaker is taking this stance.

### CONVERSATION

**M:** Can you believe the school is raising tuition?

**F:** Yeah, it's too bad, but I think it's necessary.

**M:** Really? Why do you say that?

**F:** Well, the classrooms are becoming too crowded. In one of my classes, there's over 300 students. With smaller classes, I think I'll be able to get more individual attention to help my grades.

**M:** Is that the only reason to raise tuition?

**F:** Well, another is that the research labs here are old. New equipment will improve the accuracy of our lab results.

**M:** I see what you mean.

**M:** Male Student / **F:** Female Student

### CONVERSATION NOTES

Speaker's opinion: *woman supports*

- Reason 1: *more individ. help*
- Reason 2: *new lab equip.*

 **Practice 1** The following conversation corresponds with the announcement from the previous page. Read the conversation, and fill out the note template that follows.

### CONVERSATION

**M:** This parking lot proposal is a complete joke. Most students use the bus to get around. I don't know of that many people who even have cars!

**F:** Yeah, I always see empty parking spots on campus!

**M:** Exactly! Plus, the school wants to build the lot in that grassy area where we eat our lunch every day and relax. It's so peaceful there.

**F:** That's one of my favorite places on campus. I can't believe the school is planning to do that.

**M:** I know. On top of everything, the school wants to raise our tuition to pay for the lot. I can't afford the added cost, especially not for something I don't even want.

**M:** Male Student / **F:** Female Student

### CONVERSATION NOTES

Speaker's opinion: _____

- Reason 1: _____
  _____

- Reason 2: _____
  _____

# STEP 2. PREPARE YOUR RESPONSE

**UNIVERSITY ANNOUNCEMENT**

**Tuition Increase**

The university must raise tuition next year. For five years, tuition has stayed the same. However, now we have more students. We need more professors and classrooms. We also must improve some of our facilities, which includes upgrading our laboratory equipment and computer labs.

**CONVERSATION**

**M:** Can you believe the school is raising tuition?
**F:** Yeah, it's too bad, but I think it's necessary.
**M:** Really? Why do you say that?
**F:** Well, the classrooms are becoming too crowded. In one of my classes, there's over 300 students. With smaller classes, I think I'll be able to get more individual attention to help my grades.
**M:** Is that the only reason to raise tuition?
**F:** Well, another is that the research labs here are old. New equipment will improve the accuracy of our lab results.
**M:** I see what you mean.

**M:** Male Student / **F:** Female Student

**ANNOUNCEMENT NOTES**

Announcement: ↑ *tuition next yr.*
- Reason 1: *need more prof. & classroom*
- Reason 2: *upgrade facilities*

**CONVERSATION NOTES**

Speaker's opinion: woman *supports*
- Reason 1: *more individ. help*
- Reason 2: *new lab equip.*

Once you have finished listening to the conversation, the prompt will appear on the screen.

**Prompt**

The woman expresses her opinion regarding the university's announcement. State her opinion and explain the reasons she gives for holding this opinion.

After reading the prompt, you have 30 seconds to prepare your response. During your preparation time, organize your notes so you can address the following pieces of information in your response.

1) Make sure that you can summarize the proposal in the university's announcement.

   **From Notes** → Proposal: *increase tuition next year*

2) Make sure that you know whether the speaker supports or opposes the proposal.

   **From Notes** → Speaker's opinion: *woman supports*

3) Make sure that you know why the student either supports or opposes the proposal.

   **From Notes** → Reason 1: *more individual help*

   Reason 2: *new lab equipment*

**Practice 1** Read the university's announcement and the conversation. Then prepare a Task 3 response, using the template below. Review your notes from the previous practices if necessary.

### UNIVERSITY ANNOUNCEMENT

**New Parking Lot**

The university proposes to build a new parking lot next year. There are nearly 2,000 more students here now than there were five years ago. The current parking areas cannot provide the spaces needed for the increase. The parking lot will be built over a grassy field near the center of campus, which will save students and instructors time when they walk from the parking lot to class. To pay for the parking lot, the university will increase each student's tuition by $100.

### CONVERSATION

*M: This parking lot proposal is a complete joke. Most students use the bus to get around. I don't know of that many people who even have cars!*

*F: Yeah, I always see empty parking spots on campus!*

*M: Exactly! Plus, the school wants to build the lot in that grassy area where we eat our lunch every day and relax. It's so peaceful there.*

*F: That's one of my favorite places on campus. I can't believe the school is planning to do that.*

*M: I know. On top of everything, the school wants to raise our tuition to pay for the lot. I can't afford the added cost, especially not for something I don't even want.*

*M: Male Student / F: Female Student*

1) What is proposed in the university's announcement?

   **From Notes** → Proposal: _____

2) Does the speaker support or oppose the proposal?

   **From Notes** → Speaker's opinion: _____

3) Why does the student either support or oppose the proposal?

   **From Notes** → Reason 1: _____

   Reason 2: _____

# STEP 3. DELIVER YOUR RESPONSE

Use the outline that you created in STEP 2 to guide you as you respond to the prompt.

> **Prompt**
> The woman expresses her opinion regarding the university's announcement. Briefly summarize the plan. State her opinion and explain the reasons she gives for holding this opinion.

- **Announcement Summary:** The first sentence of your response should be a summary of the university's announcement. If you have enough time during your response, explain why the university is making the campus changes that are described in the announcement.

- **Speaker's Opinion:** Then state whether the student agrees or disagrees with the university's announcement.

- **Reasons for Opinion:** Lastly, state the reasons the student gives for supporting or opposing the university's announcement.

- Include **transition words** in your response to clarify the relationships between related ideas.

| | Notes | Response |
|---|---|---|
| **Announcement Summary** | ↑ tuition next yr. | The university is proposing to raise students' tuition next year so it can hire more professors and upgrade its facilities. |
| **Speaker's Opinion** | woman supports | The woman supports the university's proposal for a couple of reasons. |
| **Reasons for Opinion** | more individ. help | *First*, the woman states that the tuition increase will allow the university to hire more professors, so students will receive more individual help with their assignments. |
| | new lab equip. | *Also*, according to the woman, the tuition increase will allow the school to purchase new lab equipment, which will improve students' lab results. |

**Practice 1** Review the following university announcement, conversation, and prompt. Then write a Task 3 response. Review your notes from the previous practices if necessary. Once you have written down your response, **say it aloud to yourself, a friend, a classmate, or a family member**.

### UNIVERSITY ANNOUNCEMENT

**New Parking Lot**

The university proposes to build a new parking lot next year. There are nearly 2,000 more students here now than there were five years ago. The current parking areas cannot provide the spaces needed for the increase. The parking lot will be built over a grassy field near the center of campus, which will save students and instructors time when they walk from the parking lot to class. To pay for the lot, the university will increase each student's tuition by $100.

### CONVERSATION

*M: This parking lot proposal is a complete joke. Most students use the bus to get around. I don't know of that many people who even have cars!*

*F: Yeah, I always see empty parking spots on campus!*

*M: Exactly! Plus, the school wants to build the lot in that grassy area where we eat our lunch every day and relax. It's so peaceful there.*

*F: That's one of my favorite places on campus. I can't believe the school is planning to do that.*

*M: I know. On top of everything, the school wants to raise our tuition to pay for the lot. I can't afford the added cost, especially not for something I don't even want.*

*M: Male Student / F: Female Student*

### Prompt

The man expresses his opinion regarding the university's announcement. Briefly summarize the plan. State his opinion and explain the reasons he gives for holding this opinion.

 **Response**

_____
_____
_____
_____
_____
_____
_____

# EXERCISE 1

Following the steps below, develop a response to the following prompt.

## STEP 1. OUTLINE YOUR RESPONSE

**UNIVERSITY ANNOUNCEMENT**

### University Requirement Changes

Next year, the university will require students to take at least one year of grammar and writing classes as well as one year of mathematics. We hope that this change will help students become well-rounded individuals rather than specialists in only one field. Additionally, these requirements will improve communication between the humanities and the sciences.

**CONVERSATION**

**M:** Hey, Diana. Don't you just hate the math and English requirements for next year?

**F:** I'm not sure how I feel about them, honestly.

**M:** I think they're ridiculous. Most students already have enough trouble fitting all their required classes into their schedule. Now they'll have to make room for more classes that don't even apply to their majors.

**F:** I guess you're right.

**M:** And students usually choose their majors based on their academic strengths. I know I chose to major in history partially because I'm terrible at math. I don't want to take a year of math classes that will ruin my hard-earned GPA.

**F:** That's true. These new requirements are kind of shortsighted.

**M:** Male Student / **F:** Female Student

**ANNOUNCEMENT NOTES**

Proposal: _____

- Reason 1: _____

- Reason 2: _____

**CONVERSATION NOTES**

Speaker's opinion: _____

- Reason 1: _____

- Reason 2: _____

*Prompt*

The man expresses his opinion regarding the university's announcement. State his opinion and explain the reasons he gives for holding this opinion.

## STEP 2. PREPARE YOUR RESPONSE            00:00:30

1) What is proposed in the university's announcement?

   **From Notes** → Proposal: _____

2) Does the speaker support or oppose the proposal?

   **From Notes** → Speaker's opinion: _____

3) Why does the student either support or oppose the proposal?

   **From Notes** → Reason 1: _____

                       Reason 2: _____

## STEP 3. DELIVER YOUR RESPONSE            00:01:00

**Response**

_____

_____

_____

_____

_____

_____

_____

# EXERCISE 1 — *Evaluation*

**Now practice saying your response aloud.** If possible, have a friend or a classmate fill out this checklist as you say your response to him or her. If you are by yourself, record and listen to your response, and then fill out the checklist below on your own.

Deliver your response within 60 seconds.

## Task 3 Response Checklist

| | Yes | Somewhat | No |
|---|---|---|---|
| • Does the speaker summarize the university's proposal? | | | |
| • Does the speaker state the student's opinion regarding the university's proposal? | | | |
| • Does the speaker list the student's two reasons for agreeing or disagreeing with the proposal? | | | |
| • Does the speaker deliver an organized response by using transition words and proper sentence structures? | | | |
| • Does the speaker deliver a coherent response by using appropriate tone and pronunciation? | | | |
| • Does the speaker finish within the time limit? | | ✕ | |

# Model Answer

| ANNOUNCEMENT NOTES | CONVERSATION NOTES |
|---|---|
| Proposal: *require 1 yr. of grammar/writing & math classes* | Speaker's opinion: *man opposes* |
| ▪ Reason 1: *create well-rounded students* | ▪ Reason 1: *too diff. to add more classes to schedule* |
| ▪ Reason 2: *improve inter-discipline comm.* | ▪ Reason 2: *unfamiliar subjects → ↓ GPA* |

1) What is proposed in the university's announcement?

   **From Notes** → Proposal: *require one year of grammar/writing and math classes*

2) Does the speaker support or oppose the proposal?

   **From Notes** → Speaker's opinion: *man opposes*

3) Why does the student either support or oppose the proposal?

   **From Notes** → Reason 1: *too difficult to add more classes to schedule*

   Reason 2: *unfamiliar subjects → lower GPA*

 **Response**

The university has announced that it'll require students to take a year of grammar, writing, and math classes in addition to the classes for their majors. The man is opposed to these changes. For one, he feels that it'll be too difficult to add these new classes to his already busy schedule. Also, he believes that requiring students to take classes in unfamiliar subjects will lower the students' GPAs.

# EXERCISE 2

Following the steps below, develop a response to the following prompt.

## STEP 1. OUTLINE YOUR RESPONSE

**UNIVERSITY ANNOUNCEMENT**

**Gymnasium Reconstruction**

The university has decided to expand the gymnasium, which is currently unable to hold the ever-growing number of students. However, this project will have two consequences: the gym will be closed during the construction, which will take approximately three months; also, the university will add 200 dollars to each student's tuition for next semester in order to cover the cost of construction.

**CONVERSATION**

**M:** Hey Julie, what do you think about the proposal for a new gym?

**F:** I know some people oppose it, but I actually think it's a good idea.

**M:** Really? Why's that?

**F:** Well, for one, the gym really is too crowded nowadays. When I go there to work out, I leave after a few minutes because all the treadmills and cardio machines are taken.

**M:** That's true. I can hardly ever find a free spot where I can lift weights.

**F:** Exactly! And 200 dollars is a small price to pay for a semester of gym access. Some people pay that much for just a few months of a gym membership.

**M:** Yeah, I guess that's a good point. Maybe I should be enthusiastic about this gym after all!

**M:** Male Student / **F:** Female Student

**ANNOUNCEMENT NOTES**

Proposal: _____

- Reason 1: _____

- Reason 2: _____

**CONVERSATION NOTES**

Speaker's opinion: _____

- Reason 1: _____

- Reason 2: _____

> **Prompt**
> The woman expresses her opinion regarding the university's announcement. State her opinion and explain the reasons she gives for holding this opinion.

## STEP 2. PREPARE YOUR RESPONSE     00:00:30

1) What is proposed in the university's announcement?

   **From Notes** → Proposal: _____

2) Does the speaker support or oppose the proposal?

   **From Notes** → Speaker's opinion: _____

3) Why does the student either support or oppose the proposal?

   **From Notes** → Reason 1: _____

   　　　　　　　　Reason 2: _____

## STEP 3. DELIVER YOUR RESPONSE     00:01:00

**Response**

_____
_____
_____
_____
_____
_____
_____
_____

CAMPUS SITUATION ♦ CHAPTER 3

# EXERCISE 2  *Evaluation*

**Now practice saying your response aloud.** If possible, have a friend or a classmate fill out this checklist as you say your response to him or her. If you are by yourself, record and listen to your response, and then fill out the checklist below on your own.

Deliver your response within 60 seconds.

## Task 3 Response Checklist

|   | Yes | Somewhat | No |
|---|---|---|---|
| • Does the speaker summarize the university's proposal? |   |   |   |
| • Does the speaker state the student's opinion regarding the university's proposal? |   |   |   |
| • Does the speaker list the student's two reasons for agreeing or disagreeing with the proposal? |   |   |   |
| • Does the speaker deliver an organized response by using transition words and proper sentence structures? |   |   |   |
| • Does the speaker deliver a coherent response by using appropriate tone and pronunciation? |   |   |   |
| • Does the speaker finish within the time limit? |   | ✗ |   |

# Model Answer

**ANNOUNCEMENT NOTES**

Proposal: *make the gym bigger*

- Consequence 1: *gym closed for 3 months*
- Consequence 2: *+$200 for tuition*

**CONVERSATION NOTES**

Speaker's opinion: *woman supports*

- Reason 1: *current gym = overcrowded*
- Reason 2: *$200/semester for gym access = very affordable*

1) What is proposed in the university's announcement?

   **From Notes →** Proposal: *make the gym bigger*

2) Does the speaker support or oppose the proposal?

   **From Notes →** Speaker's opinion: *woman supports*

3) Why does the student either support or oppose the proposal?

   **From Notes →** Reason 1: *current gym = overcrowded*

   Reason 2: *$200/semester for gym access = very affordable*

 **Response**

The university announced that the school's gymnasium will be rebuilt soon. The woman is in favor of this announcement for a couple of reasons. First, she believes the current gym is too small. She claims that she's often unable to use the gym because it's packed with students. Additionally, she feels that a 200-dollar tuition increase is very reasonable because a gym membership outside of the school would be much more expensive.

# EXERCISE 3

Following the steps below, develop a response to the following prompt.

## STEP 1. OUTLINE YOUR RESPONSE

**UNIVERSITY ANNOUNCEMENT**

**New Shuttle System**

Soon the school will introduce a shuttle system that will provide transportation throughout campus as well as access to downtown. Although there will be a 50-dollar annual fee to use this system, we believe that it will prevent students from being late to classes and give students without bikes or cars access to downtown activities.

**CONVERSATION**

**F:** I'm really excited for the new shuttle system!

**M:** Oh yeah? Why's that?

**F:** Well, I won't have to leave for class 30 minutes early and walk all the way across campus. Using the shuttle will take way less time than walking.

**M:** That's a good point; I do have to rush from class to class sometimes.

**F:** And now I'll be able to leave my car at home, so I'll save money on gas and parking fees. 50 dollars is a small price to pay for so many benefits.

**M:** You've got some good points. I didn't think about how much money the shuttle could save us.

*M: Male Student / F: Female Student*

**ANNOUNCEMENT NOTES**

Proposal: _____

_____

- Reason 1: _____

_____

- Reason 2: _____

_____

**CONVERSATION NOTES**

Speaker's opinion: _____

_____

- Reason 1: _____

_____

- Reason 2: _____

_____

> **Prompt**
> The woman expresses her opinion regarding the university's announcement. State her opinion and explain the reasons she gives for holding this opinion.

## STEP 2. PREPARE YOUR RESPONSE            00:00:30

1) What is proposed in the university's announcement?

   **From Notes** → Proposal: _____

2) Does the speaker support or oppose the proposal?

   **From Notes** → Speaker's opinion: _____

3) Why does the student either support or oppose the proposal?

   **From Notes** → Reason 1: _____

                          Reason 2: _____

## STEP 3. DELIVER YOUR RESPONSE            00:01:00

**Response**

_____

_____

_____

_____

_____

_____

_____

# EXERCISE 3 — Evaluation

**Now practice saying your response aloud.** If possible, have a friend or a classmate fill out this checklist as you say your response to him or her. If you are by yourself, record and listen to your response, and then fill out the checklist below on your own.

Deliver your response within 60 seconds.

## Task 3 Response Checklist

| | Yes | Somewhat | No |
|---|---|---|---|
| • Does the speaker summarize the university's proposal? | | | |
| • Does the speaker state the student's opinion regarding the university's proposal? | | | |
| • Does the speaker list the student's two reasons for agreeing or disagreeing with the proposal? | | | |
| • Does the speaker deliver an organized response by using transition words and proper sentence structures? | | | |
| • Does the speaker deliver a coherent response by using appropriate tone and pronunciation? | | | |
| • Does the speaker finish within the time limit? | | ✗ | |

# Model Answer

| ANNOUNCEMENT NOTES | CONVERSATION NOTES |
|---|---|
| Proposal: *new campus shuttle system ($50/yr.)* | Speaker's opinion: *woman supports* |
| • Reason 1: *↓ late to class* | • Reason 1: *quicker/easier to get to class* |
| • Reason 2: *easy downtown access* | • Reason 2: *save $ on gas & parking fees* |

1) What is proposed in the university's announcement?

   **From Notes →** Proposal: *new campus shuttle system ($50/year)*

2) Does the speaker support or oppose the proposal?

   **From Notes →** Speaker's opinion: *woman supports*

3) Why does the student either support or oppose the proposal?

   **From Notes →** Reason 1: *quicker/easier to get to class*

   Reason 2: *save money on gas and parking fees*

 **Response**

The university intends to add a shuttle system that will travel throughout campus and go downtown. The woman is in favor of the proposed shuttle system. First, the shuttle will save the woman time by allowing her to get to class quicker than walking. Moreover, she thinks that the 50-dollar annual fee for using the shuttle is acceptable because the shuttle will allow her to leave her car at home. This will save her money on gas and parking fees.

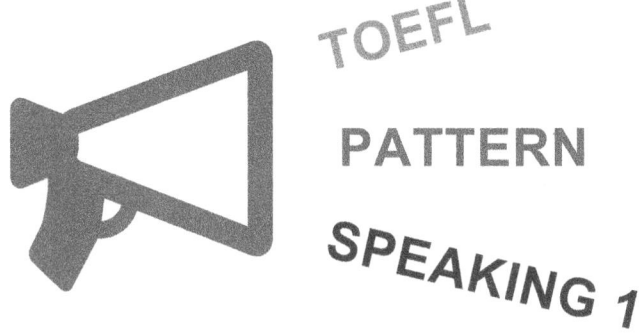

# CHAPTER 4

# Academic Course
(Reading and Listening)

# Chapter 4: Academic Course

## GENERAL BACKGROUND INFORMATION

### 1. EXPLANATION OF TASK 4

Speaking Task 4 requires that you connect the information in an academic passage to the information in a related lecture. You are scored on your ability to clearly integrate and relay important points from the passage and the lecture.

The passage provides a general definition of a term, process, or idea. The lecture covers the same topic, giving examples or detailed information to illustrate the content from the passage. The prompt asks that you combine and relay the main points from the passage and lecture.

For this task, you are given 40 to 50 seconds to read and take notes on the 75- to 100-word passage. The corresponding lecture is 60 to 90 seconds long (150 to 220 words).

After listening to the lecture, read and listen to the prompt, which stays on the screen.

> **Prompt**
> Explain how the examples discussed in the lecture illustrate the main topic presented in the passage.

You are then given 30 seconds of "Preparation Time" to prepare your response and 60 seconds of "Response Time" in which to respond.

The topics discussed in the passage and lecture are taken from a range of areas, such as psychology, history, literature, and biology. The task does not require previous knowledge of any subject.

Although you do not need to include all the information from the passage and lecture, you must provide enough information so that a listener unfamiliar with the passage and lecture would understand your response.

### 2. NECESSARY SKILLS FOR TASK 4

You must be able to:

- paraphrase subject matter from written and spoken sources
- identify and summarize major point from written and spoken sources
- convey relationships between abstract concepts and concrete information
- connect a spoken example to a written term, process, or concept

# HACKING STRATEGY

## STEP 1. Outline Your Response

- Take notes as you read the passage
- Take notes as you listen to the lecture
- Read the prompt carefully

## STEP 2. Prepare Your Response

- Summarize the passage and lecture information
- Make sure that you can fully address the prompt

## STEP 3. Deliver Your Response

- Respond with coherent sentences
- Add transition words between ideas

# HACKING STRATEGY EXAMPLE

## STEP 1. OUTLINE YOUR RESPONSE

Take notes on important information as you read the passage and listen to the corresponding lecture. Do not take notes using full sentences, as you will not have time to do so.

---

**PASSAGE**

### Science Research Terminology

When scientists describe their research, they must use very precise terms. Research terminology is like a code that indicates to others in the field exactly why and how an experiment was conducted and interpreted.

---

**LECTURE**

Now I'd like to elaborate on scientific language, the topic presented in your reading. The two terms I'll discuss today are "hypothesis" and "theory," which get mixed together in every day English.

Before doing an experiment, a scientist must make an educated guess about the outcome of that experiment; scientists call this guess a hypothesis. So, a hypothesis is based on a scientist's observations, but it's not necessarily supported by any experiments.

However, a theory presents one or more hypotheses that researchers prove through repeated experimentation. But our understanding of the world is constantly changing, so future experiments can produce results that disprove even the most well-established theory.

---

**PASSAGE NOTES**

Main Idea: *scientists → use precise terms for expt.*
- Details: *terms tell why & how expts. conducted & interpreted*

**LECTURE NOTES**

Topic: *sci. lang.*
Example 1: *hypo. = scientist's guess abt. outcome of expt.*
- Details: *based on observations, not expts.*
Example 2: *theo. = summary of hypos. supported by expt. results*
- Details: *can be disproved by more expts.*

After taking notes, carefully read the prompt, making sure that you know exactly what it asks you to do.

> **Prompt**
> Explain the differences between the two science research terms described in the lecture.

## STEP 2. PREPARE YOUR RESPONSE

During the 30-second preparation time, make sure that your notes address all the points in the prompt, and use the information in your notes to organize your response. Because you only have 30 seconds to prepare your response, do not write using complete sentences.

1) Make sure that you can summarize the main idea of the passage.
    **From Notes** → Main Idea: *scientists → use precise terms for experiments*

2) Make sure that you can summarize the lecture information.
    **From Notes** → Topic: *scientific language*
        → Example 1: *hypothesis = scientist's guess about outcome of experiment*
        → Example 2: *theory = summary of hypotheses*

3) Make sure that you can explain the differences between the two terms described in the lecture.
    **From Notes** → Details: *(P) terms may have only minor differences in meaning*
        *(L) hypothesis = based on observations, not experiments*
        *(L) theory = supported by experiments*

## STEP 3. DELIVER YOUR RESPONSE

Use the outline that you created in STEP 2 to guide you as you deliver your response. Respond using complete sentences, and add transition words to show how ideas relate to one another.

> *Scientists use very exact terms in order to express information about experiments and results. The lecture elaborates on this concept using two terms, hypothesis and theory, that are sometimes confused with each other in casual language. But these terms have very different meanings to scientists. **First**, a hypothesis is a scientist's guess about what the results of an experiment will be. **Therefore**, a hypothesis is based on observation, but it's not supported by experimental results. **Second**, a theory is one or more hypotheses that are supported by the results of one or more experiments. Theories can change if later results disprove them.*

ACADEMIC COURSE ♦ CHAPTER 4

# STEP 1A. OUTLINE YOUR RESPONSE

▶ **NOTE-TAKING STRATEGIES**

Taking notes quickly during the reading and listening portions of this task is crucial, as you can use your notes to help outline your speaking response. When taking notes, you should be able to **abbreviate**, or shorten, common words or phrases and **condense information** in order to save time.

**Tips for taking notes**

- Only write down key points/information that you will use in your response.
- Because of time constraints, do not write using full sentences.
- Make sure that you can understand your own abbreviations.

▶ **TAKING NOTES ON THE PASSAGE**

The passage will discuss an academic topic. Therefore, successful notes will state the topic and list any definitions or details that relate to the topic.

> **PASSAGE**
>
> **Parenting Styles**
>
> A *parenting style* describes the methods that a parent uses to care for and discipline his or her child. Although many other factors affect a child's development, psychologists have proven that there is a strong connection between the parenting style used during a child's upbringing and the child's emotional and social development.

> **PASSAGE NOTES**
>
> Main Idea: *parenting style → child discipline*
> - Details: *parenting style → child's emo. & soc. development*

 Read the passage and fill out the note template that follows.

**PASSAGE**

### The Harlem Renaissance

The Harlem Renaissance was a period of cultural and artistic expression for African Americans. Although the movement was primarily located in Harlem, New York, its ideas spread to many parts of the United States. The Harlem Renaissance lasted from the early 1920s until the mid 1930s.

**PASSAGE NOTES**

Main Idea: _____

- Details: _____

_____

_____

# STEP 1B. OUTLINE YOUR RESPONSE

▶ **TAKING NOTES ON THE LECTURE**

The lecture presents a topic that relates to or elaborates on the information in the passage. In your notes, identify the lecture topic and its relationship to the information in the passage.

### LECTURE

Today I'll talk about two parenting styles: authoritative and authoritarian parenting.

Authoritative parents encourage their children to think for themselves and to make many of their own choices within reason. Additionally, authoritative parents will explain rules to their children and punish them fairly and consistently if rules are broken. As a result, children learn self-control, independence, and rationality.

Contrastingly, authoritarian parents focus on enforcing discipline, often by forcing children to follow rules without explanation. Authoritarian parents are demanding, and they rarely express love or sympathy toward their children. This parenting style often causes children to have low self-esteem and difficulties in social situations.

### LECTURE NOTES

Topic: *examples of parenting styles*

Example 1: *authoritative parenting*

- Details: *children → independence, choices; punishment fair*

    *children learn control, rationality*

Example 2: *authoritarian parenting*

- Details: *rules not explained; demanding; little love*

    *children low esteem, socially bad*

**Practice 1** — The following lecture corresponds with the passage from the previous page. Read the lecture, and fill out the note template that follows.

### LECTURE

Now that the reading has given you a general idea of what happened during the Harlem Renaissance, let's look at how it influenced the music and poetry of the time.

During the Harlem Renaissance, African-American musicians began experimenting with new form of blues and jazz music. The results of these experiments interested many white composers, who began using African-American influences in their own music.

Many influential African-American authors, poets, and editors emerged during the Harlem Renaissance. The goal of many of these writers was to provide a realistic portrayal of African Americans' lives. For many authors, this meant writing about African-American hardships as well as successes.

### LECTURE NOTES

Topic: _____

Example 1: _____

- Details: _____

   _____

Example 2: _____

- Details: _____

   _____

ACADEMIC COURSE ♦ CHAPTER 4  79

# STEP 2. PREPARE YOUR RESPONSE

### PASSAGE

**Parenting Styles**

A *parenting style* describes the methods that a parent uses to care for and discipline his or her child. Although many other factors affect a child's development, psychologists have proven that there is a strong connection between the parenting style used during a child's upbringing and the child's emotional and social development.

### LECTURE

Today I'll talk about two parenting styles: authoritative and authoritarian parenting.

Authoritative parents encourage their children to think for themselves and to make many of their own choices within reason. Additionally, authoritative parents will explain rules to their children and punish them fairly and consistently if rules are broken. As a result, children learn self-control, independence, and rationality.

Contrastingly, authoritarian parents focus on enforcing discipline, often by forcing children to follow rules without explanation. Authoritarian parents are demanding, and they rarely express love or sympathy toward their children. This parenting style often causes children to have low self-esteem and difficulties in social situations.

### PASSAGE NOTES

**Main Idea:** *parenting style → child discipline*

- **Details:** *parenting style → child's emo. & soc. develop.*

### LECTURE NOTES

**Topic:** *examples of parenting styles*
**Example 1:** *authoritative parenting*
- **Details:** *children → independence, choices; punishment fair/children learn control, rationality*

**Example 2:** *authoritarian parenting*
- **Details:** *rules not explained; demanding; little love/children low esteem, socially bad*

Once you have finished listening to the lecture, the prompt will appear on the screen.

### Prompt

Describe the parenting styles discussed in the lecture, and explain how each parenting style may affect a child's behavior.

After reading the prompt, you have 30 seconds to prepare your response. During your preparation time, organize your notes so you can address the following pieces of information in your response.

1) Make sure that you can summarize main idea of the passage.

    **From Notes →** Main Idea: *parenting style → child discipline*

2) Make sure that you can summarize the lecture information.

    **From Notes →** Topic: *examples of parenting styles*

        Example 1: *authoritative parenting → independence, fair discipline*

        Example 2: *authoritarian parenting → demanding, little love*

3) Make sure that you can explain how different parenting styles can affect a child's behavior.

    **From Notes →** Details: *parenting style → child's emotional and social development*

Read the passage and the lecture. Then prepare a Task 4 response, using the template below. Review your notes from the previous practices if necessary.

> **PASSAGE**
>
> ### The Harlem Renaissance
>
> The Harlem Renaissance was a period of cultural and artistic expression for African Americans. Although the movement was primarily located in Harlem, New York, its ideas spread to many parts of the United States. The Harlem Renaissance lasted from the early 1920s until the mid 1930s.

> **LECTURE**
>
> *Now that the reading has given you a general idea of what happened during the Harlem Renaissance, let's look at how it influenced the music and poetry of the time.*
>
> *During the Harlem Renaissance, African-American musicians began experimenting with new form of blues and jazz music. The results of these experiments interested many white composers, who began using African-American influences in their own music.*
>
> *Many influential African-American authors, poets, and editors emerged during the Harlem Renaissance. The goal of many of these writers was to provide a realistic portrayal of African Americans' lives. For many authors, this meant writing about African-American hardships as well as successes.*

> **Prompt**
>
> Describe the Harlem Renaissance using examples from the lecture.

1) Summarize the main idea of the passage.

   **From Notes** → Main Idea: _____

2) Summarize the lecture information.

   **From Notes** → Topic: _____

   Example 1: _____

   Example 2: _____

3) Describe the Harlem Renaissance using examples from the lecture.

   **From Notes** → Details: _____

   _____

ACADEMIC COURSE ♦ CHAPTER 4    81

# STEP 3. DELIVER YOUR RESPONSE

Use the outline that you created in STEP 2 to guide you as you respond to the prompt.

> **Prompt**
> Describe the parenting styles discussed in the lecture, and explain how each parenting style may affect a child's behavior.

- **Passage Summary:** The first sentence of your response should be a summary of the information in the passage.
- **Lecture Topic:** Then describe the examples discussed in the lecture.
- **Passage/Lecture Relationship:** Lastly, connect the passage information to the lecture's example(s), being sure to fully respond to the prompt.
- Include **transition words** in your response to clarify the relationship between related ideas.

### Example Response

| | Notes | Response |
|---|---|---|
| **Passage Summary** | parenting style → child discipline | The reading discusses parenting styles, which are the ways a parent teaches his or her child. |
| **Lecture Topic** | authoritative parent: independence, fair discipline | The lecture talks about two different parenting styles. *First*, authoritative parenting is characterized by using fair discipline methods and encouraging a child's independence. |
| | authoritarian parenting: demanding, little love | *Second*, authoritarian parenting involves demanding expectations, and the parent usually shows little love toward the child. |
| **Passage/ Lecture Relationship** | parent style → child's emo. & soc. develop. | *Moreover*, the reading says that the parenting style used to raise a child can affect the child's emotional and social development. The lecture agrees, stating the children raised in an authoritative household are more rational while children from authoritarian environments may have low self-esteem and social problems. |

**Practice 1**

Review the following passage, lecture, and prompt. Then write a Task 4 response. Review your notes from the previous practices if necessary. Once you have written down your response, **say it aloud to yourself, a friend, a classmate, or a family member.**

### PASSAGE

#### The Harlem Renaissance

The Harlem Renaissance was a period of cultural and artistic expression for African Americans. Although the movement was primarily located in Harlem, New York, its ideas spread to many parts of the United States. The Harlem Renaissance lasted from the early 1920s until the mid 1930s.

### LECTURE

*Now that the reading has given you a general idea of what happened during the Harlem Renaissance, let's look at how it influenced the music and poetry of the time.*

*During the Harlem Renaissance, African-American musicians began experimenting with new form of blues and jazz music. The results of these experiments interested many white composers, who began using African-American influences in their own music.*

*Many influential African-American authors, poets, and editors emerged during the Harlem Renaissance. The goal of many of these writers was to provide a realistic portrayal of African Americans' lives. For many authors, this meant writing about African-American hardships as well as successes.*

### Prompt

Describe the Harlem Renaissance using examples from the lecture.

### Response

_____
_____
_____
_____
_____
_____
_____
_____

# EXERCISE 1

Following the steps below, develop a response to the following prompt.

## STEP 1. OUTLINE YOUR RESPONSE

**PASSAGE**

### Fables

*Fables* are fictional stories that give human characteristics, such as emotions and speech, to plants, animals, and forces of nature. The interactions between these characters convey a memorable moral message to the reader. Many cultures have developed unique fables to help explain cultural values.

**LECTURE**

Now let's look at a fable called "The Fir and the Bramble," which is a Greek fable about the value of confidence and uniqueness. It describes a tall fir tree that grew next to a thorny and bent bramble, which is a type of tangled shrub. One day, the fir looks down at the bramble and says, "Don't you wish to be strong and tall like me?"

The bramble responds, "No, I am proud of myself. Besides, when the woodcutter comes for tall, strong trees, I'd rather be down here."

**PASSAGE NOTES**

Main Idea: _____

_____

- Details: _____

_____

**LECTURE NOTES**

Example 1: _____

_____

- Details: _____

_____

**Prompt**

Explain how the fable presented in the lecture demonstrates the general characteristics of fables as described in the passage.

## STEP 2. PREPARE YOUR RESPONSE　　00:00:30

1) Summarize the main idea of the passage.

   **From Notes** → Main Idea: _____

2) Summarize the lecture information.

   **From Notes** → Example 1: _____

3) Explain how "The Fir and the Bramble" demonstrate the characteristics of fables.

   **From Notes** → Details: _____
   _____

## STEP 3. DELIVER YOUR RESPONSE　　00:01:00

**Response**

_____
_____
_____
_____
_____
_____
_____
_____

# EXERCISE 1  *Evaluation*

**Now practice saying your response aloud.** If possible, have a friend/classmate fill out this checklist as you say your response to him or her. If you are by yourself, record and listen to your response, and then fill out the checklist below on your own.

Deliver your response within 60 seconds.

### Task 4 Response Checklist

|  | Yes | Somewhat | No |
|---|---|---|---|
| • Does the speaker accurately summarize the concept discussed in the passage? | | | |
| • Does the speaker accurately summarize the example(s) presented in the lecture? | | | |
| • Does the speaker explain how the example(s) in the lecture relate to the concept described in the passage? | | | |
| • Does the speaker deliver an organized response by using transition words and proper sentence structures? | | | |
| • Does the speaker deliver a coherent response by using appropriate tone and pronunciation? | | | |
| • Does the speaker finish within the time limit? | | ✗ | |

# Model Answer

**PASSAGE NOTES**

Main Idea: *fable (story where non-humans are given human qualities)*

- Details: *include a moral message; explain values w/i a culture*

**LECTURE NOTES**

Example 1: *"The Fir and the Bramble" (Greek)*

- Details: *depicts talking trees*

  *moral = benefits to being small (less risk)*

1) Summarize the main idea of the passage.

   **From Notes → Main Idea:** *fable (story where non-humans are given human qualities)*

2) Summarize the lecture information.

   **From Notes → Example 1:** *"The Fir and the Bramble" (Greek)*

3) Explain how "The Fir and the Bramble" gives examples of the characteristics of fables.

   **From Notes → Details:** *depicts talking trees*

   *moral = benefits to being small (less risk)*

## Response

The passage discusses fables, which are stories in which plants and animals have human characteristics. The lecture describes a Greek fable called "The Fir and the Bramble." In this story, a bramble tells a fir tree that it's happy with its bent and thorny appearance because it won't be cut down by a woodcutter. As the passage says, fables contain moral messages and in this story, the moral is that there are benefits to having a low status, such as leading a less risky life.

# EXERCISE 2

Following the steps below, develop a response to the following prompt.

## STEP 1. OUTLINE YOUR RESPONSE

### PASSAGE

**Psychology**

Psychology is an academic field of study that examines behaviors and mental functions. Thus, many psychologists create experiments and make observations in order to comprehend the reasons for humans' actions.

### LECTURE

The study of psychology includes many different approaches to examine why people do what they do. So today, let's look at two fields of psychology: social psychology and cognitive psychology.

Social psychology analyzes how people's behaviors and feelings are affected by situations. In other words, social psychologists research how people affect one another. A social psychologist might research what causes a person to obey an order, what causes people to fall in love, what leads to bullying, and so on.

Cognitive psychology seeks to understand mental processes, or how the brain functions. For example, cognitive psychologists try to understand how people form memories, how they process language, how they filter out distractions, and how they form new concepts.

### PASSAGE NOTES

Main Idea: _____

_____

- Details: _____

_____

### LECTURE NOTES

Topic: _____

Example 1: _____

- Details: _____

Example 2: _____

- Details: _____

### Prompt

Explain how the two approaches to psychology in the lecture illustrate the definition in the passage.

## STEP 2. PREPARE YOUR RESPONSE         00:00:30

1) Summarize the main idea of the passage.

   **From Notes** → Main Idea: _____

2) Summarize the lecture information.

   **From Notes** → Topic: _____

         Example 1: _____

         Example 2: _____

3) Explain how the two approaches to psychology in the lecture illustrate the definition in the passage.

   **From Notes** → Details: _____

   _____

   _____

## STEP 3. DELIVER YOUR RESPONSE         00:01:00

**Response**

_____

_____

_____

_____

_____

_____

_____

_____

# EXERCISE 2                                                      *Evaluation*

**Now practice saying your response aloud.** If possible, have a friend/classmate fill out this checklist as you say your response to him or her. If you are by yourself, record and listen to your response, and then fill out the checklist below on your own.

Deliver your response within 60 seconds.

## Task 4 Response Checklist

|  | Yes | Somewhat | No |
|---|---|---|---|
| • Does the speaker accurately summarize the concept discussed in the passage? | | | |
| • Does the speaker accurately summarize the example(s) presented in the lecture? | | | |
| • Does the speaker explain how the example(s) in the lecture relate to the concept described in the passage? | | | |
| • Does the speaker deliver an organized response by using transition words and proper sentence structures? | | | |
| • Does the speaker deliver a coherent response by using appropriate tone and pronunciation? | | | |
| • Does the speaker finish within the time limit? | | ✗ | |

*Model Answer*

**PASSAGE NOTES**

Main Idea: _psych. (study of behaviors & the mind)_

- Details: _experiment & observe to understand human actions_

**LECTURE NOTES**

Topic: _approaches to psych._

Example 1: _soc. psych. = situations_
- Details: _i.e., what makes people obey, love, bully_

Example 2: _cog. psych. = mental processes_
- Details: _i.e., memory, language, focus_

1) Summarize the main idea of the passage.

   **From Notes →** Main Idea: _psychology = study of behaviors, mental functions_

2) Summarize the lecture information.

   **From Notes →** Topic: _approaches to psychology_

   Example 1: _social psychology = situations (exterior)_

   Example 2: _cognitive psychology = processes (interior)_

3) Explain how two approaches to psychology in the lecture illustrate the definition in the passage.

   **From Notes →** Details: _(P) psychology tries to understand reasons for human actions_

   _(L) social psychology = what makes people obey, love, bully, etc._

   _(L) cognitive psychology = how people remember, understand, focus, etc._

 **Response**

The passage defines psychology as the study of human behaviors and the mind. The lecture elaborates on this definition by explaining two approaches within the field. One is social psychology, or the study of the effect of other people and situations on behavior. The other is cognitive psychology, or the study of thought itself. Both approaches examine human behavior. For example, social psychology might look at the exterior factors that cause a person to obey another person, while cognitive psychology might look at the formations of memories or new ideas.

# EXERCISE 3

Following the steps below, develop a response to the following prompt.

## STEP 1. OUTLINE YOUR RESPONSE

### PASSAGE

**Civil Wars**

A *civil war* is a long-lasting conflict between armed forces that belong to the same nation or state. One group may begin a civil war in order to achieve total independence from the rest of the nation or to change its government's structure.

### LECTURE

Now let's look at two examples of civil wars—the first fought so one side could achieve independence; the second fought for government control.

The American Civil War was fought because the southern half of the country, which called itself the Confederacy, wanted to break away from the northern half of the country, which called itself the Union. After four years of conflict and around 750,000 deaths, the Union was able to defeat the Confederacy and force it to remain part of the U.S.

The Greek Civil War began shortly after World War II, when Communist forces supported by the Soviets tried to take government control away from conservatives, who were supported by several Western nations. For three years, the two political groups fought. Eventually, a lack of soldiers among the Communist forces contributed to the victory of the conservatives.

### PASSAGE NOTES

Main Idea: _____

_____

- Details: _____

_____

### LECTURE NOTES

Topic: _____

Example 1: _____

- Details: _____

Example 2: _____

- Details: _____

### Prompt

Using specific examples and details, explain how the two civil wars descried in the lecture relate to the description of civil wars given in the passage.

## STEP 2. PREPARE YOUR RESPONSE    00:00:30

1) Summarize the main idea of the passage.

   **From Notes** → Main Idea: _____

2) Summarize the lecture information.

   **From Notes** → Topic: _____

       Example 1: _____

       Example 2: _____

3) Explain how the types of civil wars described in the lecture relate to the passage information.

   **From Notes** → Details: _____

   _____

   _____

## STEP 3. DELIVER YOUR RESPONSE    00:01:00

**Response**

_____
_____
_____
_____
_____
_____
_____
_____

ACADEMIC COURSE ♦ CHAPTER 4   93

# EXERCISE 3　　　　　　　　　　　　　　　　　　　　*Evaluation*

**Now practice saying your response aloud.** If possible, have a friend/classmate fill out this checklist as you say your response to him or her. If you are by yourself, record and listen to your response, and then fill out the checklist below on your own.

Deliver your response within 60 seconds.

## Task 4 Response Checklist

|  | Yes | Somewhat | No |
|---|---|---|---|
| • Does the speaker accurately summarize the concept discussed in the passage? |  |  |  |
| • Does the speaker accurately summarize the example(s) presented in the lecture? |  |  |  |
| • Does the speaker explain how the example(s) in the lecture relate to the concept described in the passage? |  |  |  |
| • Does the speaker deliver an organized response by using transition words and proper sentence structures? |  |  |  |
| • Does the speaker deliver a coherent response by using appropriate tone and pronunciation? |  |  |  |
| • Does the speaker finish within the time limit? |  | ✕ | ✕ |

*Model Answer*

**PASSAGE NOTES**

Main Idea: *civil wars (when a nation or state is at war w/ itself)*

- Details: *one side → change gov./achieve independence*

**LECTURE NOTES**

Topic: *types of civil wars*

Example 1: *U.S. Civil War (Union vs. Confeds.)*
- Details: *Confeds. (wanted own nation) → Union won (Confeds. to rejoin U.S.)*

Example 2: *Greek Civil War (Comm. vs. conserv.)*
- Details: *Comm. (wanted to run gov.) → not enough soldiers → lost*

1) Summarize the main idea of the passage.

   **From Notes →** Main Idea: *civil wars (when a nation or state is at war with itself)*

2) Summarize the lecture information.

   **From Notes →** Topic: *types of civil wars*

   Example 1: *U.S. Civil War (Union vs. Confederacy)*

   Example 2: *Greek Civil War (Communists vs. conservatives)*

3) Explain how the types of civil wars described in the lecture relate to the passage information.

   **From Notes →** Details: *(P) one side → change government/achieve independence*

   *(L) Confederates (wanted own nation) → Union won (Confederates to rejoin U.S.)*

   *(L) Communists (wanted to run government) → not enough soldiers → lost*

 **Response**

The passage discusses civil wars, which occur when a nation or state is at war with itself. According to the passage, some civil wars begin when one side wants to achieve independence. For example, the lecture states that the American Civil War occurred because the Confederates, who were from the southern U.S., wanted to break away from the rest of the nation. Civil wars also occur because one side wants to change the way a nation's government is run. For example, the Greek Civil War began because Communist forces wanted to take over the government.

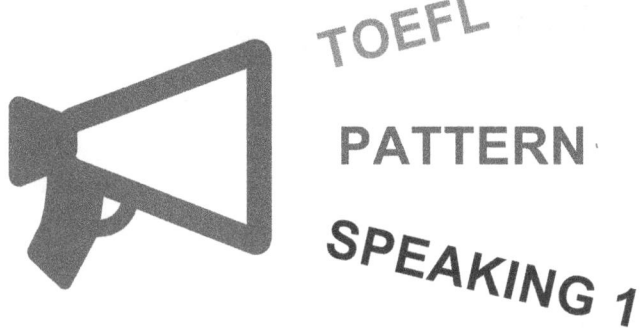

# CHAPTER 5

# Campus Situation
### (Listening)

# Chapter 5: Campus Situation

## GENERAL BACKGROUND INFORMATION

### 1. EXPLANATION OF TASK 5

Task 5 requires you to listen to a short conversation that one might hear in a university setting. The conversation will be between a student and another student, a professor, or a university employee.

Some common conversation topics include:

- academic problems (e.g. bad grades, difficulty deciding on a major)
- scheduling conflicts or absences
- financial difficulties

In the conversation, a student will describe a problem that he or she is having, and the other speaker will provide two possible solutions.

After listening to the conversation, you will be given a prompt related to what you have heard. The prompt appears on your computer screen and is read aloud by a narrator.

> **Prompt**
> The speakers discuss two solutions to the man's/woman's problem. Explain what the man's/woman's problem is. Then state which solution you prefer and explain your preference.

When providing a preferred solution in your response, you can either use one of the solutions from the conversation or come up with your own solution. Similarly, when producing reasons to support your preferred solution, you can either use the reasons stated in the conversation or create your own.

After reading the prompt, you have 20 seconds of "Preparation Time" to prepare your response. At the end, you will hear a short beep. The clock then changes to "Response Time" and begins to count down.

You have 60 seconds in which to respond. At the end of the 60 seconds, the recording ends and a new message alerts you that the response time is over.

You may take notes while listening to the conversation and during your preparation time. You also may check your notes when responding to the question.

### 2. NECESSARY SKILLS FOR TASK 5

You must be able to:

- understand information from spoken sources regarding campus-based subject matter
- identify and summarize major points and important details from spoken sources
- discuss the connection between issues and their proposed solutions

# HACKING STRATEGY

### STEP 1. Outline Your Response

- Take notes as you listen to the conversation
- Read the prompt carefully

### STEP 2. Prepare Your Response

- Explain the student's problem
- State which solution you prefer and why you prefer it

### STEP 3. Deliver Your Response

- Respond with coherent sentences
- Add transition words between ideas

# *HACKING STRATEGY EXAMPLE*

## STEP 1. OUTLINE YOUR RESPONSE

Take notes on important information as you listen to the conversation. Do not take notes using full sentences, as you will not have time to do so.

**CONVERSATION**

**A**: You look upset. Can I help you with something?

**MS**: My computer is broken, and I can't afford a new one right now. What should I do?

**A**: I'm sorry to hear that. Well, we do have a large computer lab where you can do your work. The lab even has printers and copiers. And it's open all day every day.

**MS**: Thanks, that might work. But I live off-campus, so it might be impossible for me to get to the computer lab at night, especially since buses don't run that late.

**A**: Hmm, that could be a problem. You could also get a part-time job to save up for a new laptop.

**MS**: That's true. But I don't know how that's going to work with my current school schedule.

**A**: Well, one way or another, you're probably going to need computer access to complete your school work.

**A**: Advisor / **MS**: Male Student

**CONVERSATION NOTES**

Problem: *computer broken, can't afford new one*

- Solution 1: *use computer lab*
- Solution 2: *get a job to save $ for new one*

After taking notes, carefully read the prompt, making sure that you know exactly what it asks you to do.

> **Prompt**
>
> The advisor and the student talk about two solutions to the student's problem. Explain what the student's problem is. Then state which solution you prefer and explain your preference.

## STEP 2. PREPARE YOUR RESPONSE

During the 20-second preparation time, make sure that your notes address all the points in the prompt, and use the information in your notes to organize your response. Because you only have 20 seconds to prepare your response, do not write using complete sentences.

1) Make sure that you can summarize the student's problem.
    **From Notes →** Problem: *computer broken, can't afford new one*

2) Make sure that you can identify which of the two proposed solutions you prefer.
    Preferred solution: *get a job to save money for new one*

3) Make sure that you can give two reasons explaining why you prefer this solution.
    Reason 1: *avoid having to go to campus every day*
    Reason 2: *use everywhere*

## STEP 3. DELIVER YOUR RESPONSE

Use the outline that you created in STEP 2 to guide you as you deliver your response. Respond using complete sentences, and add transition words to show how ideas relate to one another.

*The issue discussed in the conversation is that the student's computer is broken, and he says he doesn't have enough money to buy a new one. The advisor suggests that he either use the university's computer lab or get a job and buy a new computer. I think he should get a job so he can buy a new computer.* ***First****, if he buys his own computer, he won't have to go all the way to campus to use the computer lab, and he'll be more likely to complete his assignments.* ***Additionally****, buying his own computer will allow him to do his assignments anywhere. Even if he's far away from the university, he can still do research for his assignments.*

# STEP 1. OUTLINE YOUR RESPONSE

▶ **NOTE-TAKING STRATEGIES**

Taking notes quickly while listening to the conversation is crucial, as you can use your notes to help outline your speaking response. When taking notes, you should be able to **abbreviate**, or shorten, common words or phrases and **condense information** in order to save time.

**Tips for taking notes**

- Only write down key points/information that you will use in your response.
- Because of time constraints, do not write using full sentences.
- Make sure that you can understand your own abbreviations.

▶ **TAKING NOTES ON THE CONVERSATION**

When taking notes, be sure to identify the **problem** and whom it affects. Then write down the **two solutions** proposed and mark which solution you think will be more effective.

---

**CONVERSATION**

**F:** So, did you find a summer job yet?

**M:** No. And I've looked everywhere in this city.

**F:** You should try the career center. They have a special section for summer jobs.

**M:** Really? I didn't know that.

**F:** Or you could work with me in my parents' restaurant.

**M:** Oh, right. They always need summer help.

**F:** And the tips are great. Last summer I was able to save quite a bit.

**F:** Female Student / **M:** Male Student

**CONVERSATION NOTES**

Problem: *man can't find summer job*

- Solution 1: *check career center*
- Solution 2: *work @ woman's fam. rest.*

**Practice 1** Read the conversation and fill out the note template that follows.

### CONVERSATION

**F:** What's wrong, Ted?

**M:** I don't have the money to pay for school next quarter. What am I going to do, Lana?

**F:** I'm so sorry. But don't worry; there are options.

**M:** Like what?

**F:** You could take out a student loan. You can get that right away, and monthly payments are low.

**M:** Well, I'll think about it.

**F:** Or you could apply for some scholarships.

**M:** I did that last year and didn't get any.

**F:** Right, it's more risky. But if you do get some scholarship money, you never have to pay it back.

*F: Female Student / M: Male Student*

### CONVERSATION NOTES

Problem: _____

- Solution 1: _____

- Solution 2: _____

# STEP 2. PREPARE YOUR RESPONSE

> **CONVERSATION**
>
> **F:** So, did you find a summer job yet?
>
> **M:** No. And I've looked everywhere in this city.
>
> **F:** You should try the career center. They have a special section for summer jobs.
>
> **M:** Really? I didn't know that.
>
> **F:** Or you could work with me in my parents' restaurant.
>
> **M:** Oh, right. They always need summer help.
>
> **F:** And the tips are great. Last summer I was able to save quite a bit.

**F:** Female Student / **M:** Male Student

> **CONVERSATION NOTES**
>
> Problem: *man can't find summer job*
>
> - Solution 1: *check career center*
> - Solution 2: *work @ woman's fam. rest.*

After taking notes on the conversation, carefully read the prompt that appears on the screen. Make sure that you understand exactly what the prompt is asking you to do.

> **Prompt**
>
> The students talk about two solutions to the man's problem. Explain what the man's problem is. Then state which solution you prefer and explain your preference.

After reading the prompt, you have 20 seconds to prepare your response. During your preparation time, organize your notes so you can address the following pieces of information in your response.

1) Make sure that you can summarize the student's problem.

   **From Notes** → Problem: *man can't find summer job*

2) Make sure that you can identify which of the two proposed solutions you prefer.

   **From Notes** → Preferred solution: *work at woman's family restaurant*

3) Make sure that you can give two reasons explaining why you prefer this solution.

   **From Notes** → Reason 1: *job available right away*

   Reason 2: *save lots of money*

**Practice 1** — Review the following conversation. Then prepare a Task 5 response, using the template below. Review your notes from the previous page if necessary.

### CONVERSATION

**F:** What's wrong, Ted?

**M:** I don't have the money to pay for school next quarter. What am I going to do, Lana?

**F:** I'm so sorry. But don't worry; there are options.

**M:** Like what?

**F:** You could take out a student loan. You can get that right away, and monthly payments are low.

**M:** Well, I'll think about it.

**F:** Or you could apply for some scholarships.

**M:** I did that last year and didn't get any.

**F:** Right, it's more risky. But if you do get some scholarship money, you never have to pay it back.

*F: Female Student / M: Male Student*

### Prompt

The students discuss two solutions to the man's problem. Explain what the man's problem is. Then state which solution you prefer and explain your preference.

1) Summarize the student's problem.

   **From Notes →** Problem: _____

2) Identify which of the two proposed solutions your prefer.

   Preferred solution: _____

3) Give two reasons explaining why you prefer this solution.

   Reason 1: _____

   Reason 2: _____

# STEP 3. DELIVER YOUR RESPONSE

Use the outline that you created in STEP 2 to guide you as you respond to the prompt.

> **Prompt**
> The students talk about two solutions to the man's problem. Explain what the man's problem is. Then state which solution you prefer and explain your preference.

- **Student's Problem:** The first sentence of your response should be a summary of the student's problem.

- **Preferred Solution:** Then state which of the two solutions presented in the conversation you prefer.

- **Reasons for Preference:** Lastly, give two reasons stating why you prefer this solution. You can either use reasons from the conversation or come up with reasons of your own.

- When you respond, include **transition words** where they are appropriate. Doing so will make one idea flow smoothly into the next. See below for a sample of a completed response.

| | Notes | Response |
|---|---|---|
| **Student's Problem** | man can't find summer job | The problem discussed by the two students is that the man can't find a summer job. |
| **Preferred Solution** | work @ woman's fam. rest. | I believe the man should work with the woman at her parents' restaurant. |
| **Reasons for Preference** | job avail. right away | *For one*, the restaurant job is already available, and the woman makes it seem like the man can begin working right away. |
| | save lots of $ | *Additionally*, the woman claims that she made a lot of money in tips. Since saving money is a major concern for many college students, the man should accept the job. |

**Practice 1**

Review the following conversation and prompt. Then write a Task 5 response. Review your notes from the previous practices if necessary. Once you have written down your response, **say it aloud to yourself, a friend, a classmate, or a family member**.

### CONVERSATION

**F:** What's wrong, Ted?

**M:** I don't have the money to pay for school next quarter. What am I going to do, Lana?

**F:** I'm so sorry. But don't worry; there are options.

**M:** Like what?

**F:** You could take out a student loan. You can get that right away, and monthly payments are low.

**M:** Well, I'll think about it.

**F:** Or you could apply for some scholarships.

**M:** I did that last year and didn't get any.

**F:** Right, it's more risky. But if you do get some scholarship money, you never have to pay it back.

**F:** Female Student / **M:** Male Student

### Prompt

The students discuss two solutions to the man's problem. Explain what the man's problem is. Then state which solution you prefer and explain your preference.

### Response

# EXERCISE 1

Following the steps below, develop a response to the following prompt.

## STEP 1. OUTLINE YOUR RESPONSE

**CONVERSATION**

**M:** I'm so embarrassed! I fell asleep in my early morning class again.

**F:** Oh, that's kind of embarrassing. When did you go to bed last night?

**M:** Not until 1 a.m.

**F:** Well, that might be the problem. If you went to sleep earlier, you might not have trouble staying awake early in the morning.

**M:** I know, but I always have so much studying to do; studying almost always keeps me up late.

**F:** If you can't get your studying done earlier, maybe you need to take classes that start later in the day. That way you can get plenty of sleep.

**M:** I'll keep that in mind. I just worry that taking later classes will force me to stay up even later, just so I can catch up on my studies!

**M:** Male Student / **F:** Female Student

**CONVERSATION NOTES**

Problem: _____

- Solution 1: _____
- Solution 2: _____

**Prompt**

The students talk about two solutions to the man's problem. Explain what the man's problem is. Then state which solution you prefer and explain your preference.

## STEP 2. PREPARE YOUR RESPONSE          `00:00:20`

1) Summarize the student's problem.

   **From Notes** → Problem: _____

2) Identify which of the two proposed solutions you prefer.

   Preferred solution: _____

3) Give two reasons explaining why you prefer this solution.

   Reason 1: _____

   Reason 2: _____

## STEP 3. DELIVER YOUR RESPONSE          `00:01:00`

🔊 **Response**

_____
_____
_____
_____
_____
_____
_____
_____
_____
_____
_____

# EXERCISE 1　　　　　　　　　　　　*Evaluation*

**Now practice saying your response aloud.** If possible, have a friend/classmate fill out this checklist as you say your response to him or her. If you are by yourself, record and listen to your response, and then fill out the checklist below on your own.

Deliver your response within 60 seconds.

### Task 5 Response Checklist

|  | Yes | Somewhat | No |
|---|---|---|---|
| • Does the speaker explain the problem discussed in the conversation? | | | |
| • Does the speaker state which of the two proposed solutions he or she prefers? | | | |
| • Does the speaker explain why he or she selected this preferred solution? | | | |
| • Does the speaker deliver an organized response by using transition words and proper sentence structures? | | | |
| • Does the speaker deliver a coherent response by using appropriate tone and pronunciation? | | | |
| • Does the speaker finish within the time limit? | | | |

## Model Answer

### CONVERSATION NOTES

Problem: *man falls asleep in class, studying too late*

- Solution 1: *go to sleep earlier*
- Solution 2: *take later classes*

1) Summarize the student's problem.

   **From Notes →** Problem: *man falls asleep in class, studying too late*

2) Identify which of the two proposed solutions you prefer.

   Preferred solution: *take later classes*

3) Give two reasons explaining why you prefer this solution.

   Reason 1: *get more sleep in morning*

   Reason 2: *can study before classes*

 **Response**

The man's problem is that he often falls asleep during class because he stays up late studying. The woman proposes that he either go to sleep earlier each night or take classes that start later in the day. I think the man should take later classes. For one, staying up late at night and getting up late in the morning seem to be his normal sleeping cycle. And by getting more sleep in the morning, he may be more energized and get his studying done more quickly later in the day.

# EXERCISE 2

Following the steps below, develop a response to the following prompt.

## STEP 1. OUTLINE YOUR RESPONSE

### CONVERSATION

**M:** Hey, Laura. You look troubled.

**F:** Yeah, I have to decide on a major by the end of this year, but I can't decide between engineering and sociology.

**M:** Hmm. That does sound like a tough decision. Have you tried talking to an academic advisor? That's what I did when I was deciding on a major. It really helped me figure out my options.

**F:** I haven't done that yet. That's a helpful suggestion.

**M:** And you know, if that doesn't work out, you could always try to double major. I hear it's a lot of work, but I think you can manage it if you really enjoy studying both subjects.

**F:** That does sound difficult, but maybe you're right. I'll have to give this issue some more thought.

**M:** Male Student / **F:** Female Student

### CONVERSATION NOTES

Problem: _____

- Solution 1: _____

- Solution 2: _____

### Prompt

The students talk about two solutions to the female student's problem. Explain what the female student's problem is. Then state which solution you prefer and explain your preference.

## STEP 2. PREPARE YOUR RESPONSE

00:00:20

1) Summarize the student's problem.

   **From Notes** → Problem: _____

2) Identify which of the two proposed solutions you prefer.

   Preferred solution: _____

3) Give two reasons explaining why you prefer this solution.

   Reason 1: _____

   Reason 2: _____

## STEP 3. DELIVER YOUR RESPONSE

00:01:00

**Response**

_____
_____
_____
_____
_____
_____
_____
_____
_____

# EXERCISE 2  *Evaluation*

**Now practice saying your response aloud.** If possible, have a friend/classmate fill out this checklist as you say your response to him or her. If you are by yourself, record and listen to your response, and then fill out the checklist below on your own.

Deliver your response within 60 seconds.

## Task 5 Response Checklist

| | Yes | Somewhat | No |
|---|---|---|---|
| • Does the speaker explain the problem discussed in the conversation? | | | |
| • Does the speaker state which of the two proposed solutions he or she prefers? | | | |
| • Does the speaker explain why he or she selected this preferred solution? | | | |
| • Does the speaker deliver an organized response by using transition words and proper sentence structures? | | | |
| • Does the speaker deliver a coherent response by using appropriate tone and pronunciation? | | | |
| • Does the speaker finish within the time limit? | | ✗ | |

# Model Answer

**CONVERSATION NOTES**

Problem: *woman can't decide on a major*

Solution 1: *talk to advisor*

Solution 2: *double major (engineering & soc.)*

1) Summarize the student's problem.

   **From Notes →** Problem: *woman can't decide on a major*

2) Identify which of the two proposed solutions you prefer.

   Preferred solution: *talk to advisor*

3) Give two reasons explaining why you prefer this solution.

   Reason 1: *beneficial to get a professional's opinion*

   Reason 2: *can double major later*

 **Response**

According to the conversation, the woman can't decide on a major, but she has to by the end of the year. Of the two proposed solutions, I think the woman should talk to an advisor before deciding on a major. One reason this is the best solution is that she may not have considered the consequences of her decision, so it'd be beneficial for her to get a professional advisor's assistance. Moreover, pursuing a double major may prove overwhelming. She can always decide to add another major later after making some progress in either engineering or sociology.

# EXERCISE 3

Following the steps below, develop a response to the following prompt.

## STEP 1. OUTLINE YOUR RESPONSE

**CONVERSATION**

**FS:** Excuse me, professor, can I speak with you for a minute?

**P:** Of course, what can I help you with?

**FS:** I really enjoy your class, but I find some of the material almost impossible to understand. I've been studying more and more, but I can't seem to get my grade up.

**P:** I'm sorry to hear that. This subject can be challenging for many students. Perhaps you should choose to take the class as "pass or no pass" rather than for a letter grade. That might put less stress on you.

**FS:** Thank you for the suggestion, but I'm afraid the graduate schools I apply to might require a letter grade for this class.

**P:** Well, in that case, you should attend my weekly office hours. It'll take up some of your time, but I can address any specific questions you have there.

**FS:** Thanks for the advice!

**FS:** Female Student / **P:** Professor

**CONVERSATION NOTES**

Problem: _____

• Solution 1: _____

• Solution 2: _____

**Prompt**

The student and the professor discuss two solutions to the student's problem. Explain what the student's problem is. Then state which solution you prefer and explain your preference.

## STEP 2. PREPARE YOUR RESPONSE  00:00:20

1) Summarize the student's problem.

   **From Notes** → Problem: _____

2) Identify which of the two proposed solutions you prefer.

   Preferred solution: _____

3) Give two reasons explaining why you prefer this solution.

   Reason 1: _____

   Reason 2: _____

## STEP 3. DELIVER YOUR RESPONSE  00:01:00

**Response**

_____
_____
_____
_____
_____
_____
_____
_____
_____
_____

# EXERCISE 3 — *Evaluation*

**Now practice saying your response aloud.** If possible, have a friend/classmate fill out this checklist as you say your response to him or her. If you are by yourself, record and listen to your response, and then fill out the checklist below on your own.

Deliver your response within 60 seconds.

## Task 5 Response Checklist

|  | Yes | Somewhat | No |
|---|---|---|---|
| • Does the speaker explain the problem discussed in the conversation? |  |  |  |
| • Does the speaker state which of the two proposed solutions he or she prefers? |  |  |  |
| • Does the speaker explain why he or she selected this preferred solution? |  |  |  |
| • Does the speaker deliver an organized response by using transition words and proper sentence structures? |  |  |  |
| • Does the speaker deliver a coherent response by using appropriate tone and pronunciation? |  |  |  |
| • Does the speaker finish within the time limit? |  | ✕ |  |

*Model Answer*

### CONVERSATION NOTES

Problem: *woman's class too diff.*

- Solution 1: *take the class P/NP*
- Solution 2: *attend prof.'s office hours*

1) Summarize the student's problem.

   **From Notes** → Problem: *woman's class too difficult*

2) Identify which of the two proposed solutions you prefer.

   Preferred solution: *attend professor's office hours*

3) Give two reasons explaining why you prefer this solution.

   Reason 1: *get one-on-one help*

   Reason 2: *better option for grad school*

### Response

The student's issue is that she finds the professor's class too difficult. In my opinion, the woman should attend the professor's office hours and try to bring her grade up for a couple of reasons. First, going to the office hours will give her opportunities to get one-on-one help with any difficult concepts. She should be able to do well in class if she can ask the professor about any confusing information. Moreover, as the woman says, taking the class for a letter grade will look better on her college transcript, so attending office hours is definitely the wiser decision.

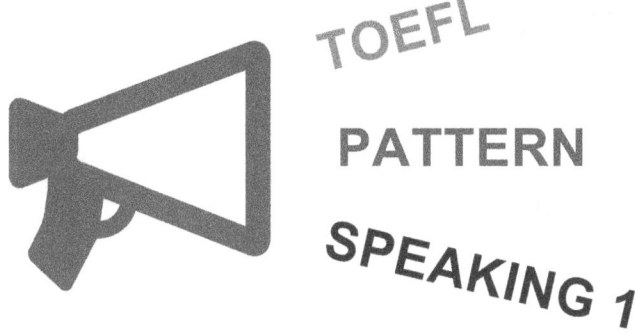

# CHAPTER 6

# Academic Course
(Listening)

# Chapter 6: Academic Course

## GENERAL BACKGROUND INFORMATION

### 1. EXPLANATION OF TASK 6

Speaking Task 6 requires you to listen to a brief lecture on an academic subject. The lecture lasts about 90 to 120 seconds and is about 230 to 280 words. The lecture describes a term or concept using academic details or examples. Topics are taken from a range of fields in the life sciences, humanities, social sciences, and physical sciences.

After you listen to the lecture, instructions will inform you to get ready to respond to the prompt. The prompt will then appear on screen and be read aloud by a narrator.

The task 6 prompt will ask you to describe the main concept or issue of the lecture and use points or examples from the lecture to support the main idea.

> **Prompt**
> Using points and examples from the lecture, explain the topic discussed in the lecture.

After listening to the prompt, begin preparing your response. A clock below the prompt will count down. You will have 20 seconds to prepare. At the end, you will hear a short beep.

The clock then changes to "Response Time" and begins to count down. You have 60 seconds to respond. At the end of the 60 seconds, the recording ends and a new message alerts you that the response time is over.

You will need to use citation language, summarizing, paraphrasing, and transitions for this task.

### 2. NECESSARY SKILLS FOR TASK 6

You must be able to:

- identify and summarize major points from a spoken source of information
- paraphrase information from spoken sources of information
- relate specific examples to a general topic generated from spoken sources of information

# HACKING STRATEGY

### STEP 1. OUTLINE YOUR RESPONSE

- Take notes as you listen to the lecture
- Read the prompt carefully

### STEP 2. PREPARE YOUR RESPONSE

- Summarize the lecture's main idea
- State how the examples in the lecture relate to the main idea or to each other

### STEP 3. DELIVER YOUR RESPONSE

- Respond with coherent sentences
- Add transition words between ideas

# HACKING STRATEGY EXAMPLE

## STEP 1. OUTLINE YOUR RESPONSE

Take notes on important information as you listen to the lecture. Do not take notes using full sentences, as you will not have time to do so.

> **LECTURE**
>
> **Introduction to Grammar**
>
> Grammar is usually described as the set of rules used in a language. But the rules of grammar you follow in day-to-day conversations differ from the rules of grammar you learned in school. So today we'll talk about two kinds of grammar: descriptive grammar and prescriptive grammar.
>
> As the name suggests, descriptive grammar describes the ways that people actually use language and grammar in their daily lives. So the slang and grammatical structures you use when you're talking to your friends are part of descriptive grammar. Those who study descriptive grammar are called linguists.
>
> On the other hand, prescriptive grammar, which is "prescribed" by educators and editors, looks at how one should use a language. So the rules of grammar you studied in school fall under prescriptive grammar. The basis of this type of grammar is that there's a "right" and "wrong" way to use language.

> **LECTURE NOTES**
>
> **Main Idea:** *diff. types of grammar*
>
> - **Subtopic 1:** *descript. grammar = daily life grammar*
>
>     **Details:** *ex. grammar in normal conv.*
>
>     → *linguists*
>
> - **Subtopic 2:** *prescript. grammar = proper grammar use*
>
>     **Details:** *ex. grammar learned in school; "right" vs. "wrong" grammar*
>
>     → *educators/editors*

After taking notes, carefully read the prompt, making sure that you know exactly what it asks you to do.

> **Prompt**
> Using reasons and details from the lecture, explain the two types of grammar discussed by the lecturer.

## STEP 2. PREPARE YOUR RESPONSE

During the 20-second preparation time, make sure that your notes address all the points in the prompt, and use the information in your notes to organize your response. Because you only have 20 seconds to prepare your response, do not write using complete sentences.

1) Make sure that you can summarize the main idea of the lecture.
   **From Notes** → Main Idea: *different types of grammar*

2) Make sure that you can explain the first subtopic presented in the lecture.
   **From Notes** → Subtopic 1: *descriptive grammar = daily life grammar, grammar in normal conversation (linguists)*

3) Make sure that you can explain the second subtopic presented in the lecture.
   **From Notes** → Subtopic 2: *prescriptive grammar = proper grammar use; "right" vs. "wrong" grammar (teachers/editors)*

## STEP 3. DELIVER YOUR RESPONSE

Use the outline that you created in STEP 2 to guide you as you deliver your response. Respond using complete sentences, and add transition words to show how ideas relate to one another.

*The lecture discusses the idea that people use grammar differently depending on the situation.* **First**, *the lecture discusses descriptive grammar, or the study of the way people use language in their everyday speech, including slang. Studying and describing the everyday use of a language are what a linguist does. Grammar can also be described as standard rules about how language is "supposed" to be used. This is called prescriptive grammar.* **For instance**, *editors use prescriptive grammar when they proofread.*

# STEP 1. OUTLINE YOUR RESPONSE

▶ **NOTE-TAKING STRATEGIES**

Taking notes quickly while listening to the lecture is crucial, as you can use your notes to help outline your speaking response. When taking notes, you should be able to **abbreviate**, or shorten, common words or phrases and **condense information** in order to save time.

Tips for taking notes:

- Only write down key points/information that you will use in your response.
- Because of time constraints, do not write in full sentences.
- Make sure that you can understand your own abbreviations.

▶ **TAKING NOTES ON THE LECTURE**

When taking notes on the lecture, be sure to identify the **main idea** of the lecture. Then take notes on the **two subtopics** that relate to or elaborate on the main idea.

---

**LECTURE**

### Objective and Subjective Statements

In all academic fields of study, it's important to understand whether something can be proven true or not. To do so, we must understand whether a claim is objective or subjective.

An objective statement is one that can be proven true or false based on some commonly accepted method. For example, consider the statement, "Many people around the world eat insects." This statement can be verified, possibly by sending a survey to a random sample of people from around the world. Therefore, it is an objective statement.

Subjective statements can't be proven true or false because they're opinions. The statement, "Bugs are delicious" is a subjective statement because it can't be proven universally true. Although the statement is true to the speaker, many people will disagree and claim, "Eating bugs is disgusting."

**LECTURE NOTES**

Main Idea: *determine if a thing can be proven true*

- Subtopic 1: *obj. statement = provable*

    Details: *ex. insect eaters*

- Subtopic 2: *subj. statement = opinion*

    Details: *ex. bugs delicious/disgusting*

**Practice 1** Read the lecture and fill out the note template that follows.

### LECTURE

**Animal Migration**

Each year, thousands of animal species travel from one region to another in a process known as "migration." Almost all animals migrate to find food, a better climate, or a place to breed.

Let's take a look at the migration of humpback whales. During the summer, humpback whales search for food in the cold, nutrient-rich waters near the north and south poles. But these waters are too cold for breeding, so during the winter months, the whales travel to the warmer waters near the equator to breed. This roundtrip journey can total about 25,000 kilometers.

Pacific salmon also undergo a difficult migration. After reaching adulthood in the ocean, the salmon will travel to freshwater rivers, where they swim upstream so they can breed in the same places they were born. The few salmon that survive the difficult journey die after breeding.

### LECTURE NOTES

Main Idea: _____

- Subtopic 1: _____

    Details: _____

- Subtopic 2: _____

    Details: _____

# STEP 2. PREPARE YOUR RESPONSE

### LECTURE

**Objective and Subjective Statements**

In all academic fields of study, it's important to understand whether something can be proven true or not. To do so, we must understand whether a claim is objective or subjective.

An objective statement is one that can be proven true or false based on some commonly accepted method. For example, consider the statement, "Many people around the world eat insects." This statement can be verified, possibly by sending a survey to a random sample of people from around the world. Therefore, it is an objective statement.

Subjective statements can't be proven true or false because they're opinions. The statement, "Bugs are delicious" is a subjective statement because it can't be proven universally true. Although the statement is true to the speaker, many people will disagree and claim, "Eating bugs is disgusting."

### LECTURE NOTES

**Main Idea:** *determine if a thing can be proven true*
- **Subtopic 1:** *obj. statement = provable*
    - **Details:** *ex. insect eaters*
- **Subtopic 2:** *subj. statement = opinion*
    - **Details:** *ex. bugs delicious/disgusting*

After taking notes on the lecture, carefully read the prompt that appears on the screen. Make sure that you understand exactly what the prompt is asking you to do.

### Prompt

Using examples from the lecture, explain why researchers must distinguish objective statements from subjective statements.

After reading the prompt, you have 20 seconds to prepare your response. During your preparation time, organize your notes so you can address the following pieces of information in your response.

1) Make sure that you can summarize the main idea of the lecture.

   **From Notes** → **Main Idea:** *determine if a thing can be proven true*

2) Make sure that you can explain the first subtopic presented in the lecture.

   **From Notes** → **Subtopic 1:** *objective statement = provable (ex. insect eaters)*

3) Make sure that you can explain the second subtopic presented in the lecture.

   **From Notes** → **Subtopic 2:** *subjective statement = opinion (ex. bugs delicious/disgusting)*

**PRACTICE 1** Review the following lecture. Then prepare a Task 6 response, using the template below. Review your notes from the previous page if necessary.

> **LECTURE**
>
> ### Animal Migration
>
> *Each year, thousands of animal species travel from one region to another in a process known as "migration." Almost all animals migrate to find food, a better climate, or a place to breed.*
>
> *Let's take a look at the migration of humpback whales. During the summer, humpback whales search for food in the cold, nutrient-rich waters near the north and south poles. But these waters are too cold for breeding, so during the winter months, the whales travel to the warmer waters near the equator to breed. This roundtrip journey can total about 25,000 kilometers.*
>
> *Pacific salmon also undergo a difficult migration. After reaching adulthood in the ocean, the salmon will travel to freshwater rivers, where they swim upstream so they can breed in the same places they were born. The few salmon that survive the difficult journey die after breeding.*

> **Prompt**
>
> Using examples from the lecture, explain some of the reasons that animals migrate.

1) Summarize the main idea of the lecture.

   **From Notes → Main Idea:** _____

2) Explain the first subtopic presented in the lecture.

   **From Notes → Subtopic 1:** _____

   _____

   _____

3) Explain the second subtopic presented in the lecture.

   **From Notes → Subtopic 2:** _____

   _____

   _____

# STEP 3. DELIVER YOUR RESPONSE

Use the outline that you created in STEP 2 to guide you as you respond to the prompt.

> **Prompt**
> Using examples from the lecture, explain why researchers must distinguish between objective and subjective statements.

- **Lecture Main Idea:** The first sentence of your response should be a summary of the main idea from the lecture.

- **Summary of Subtopic 1:** Then describe the first subtopic of the lecture, being sure to relate it to the main idea.

- **Summary of Subtopic 2:** Lastly, describe the second subtopic, being sure to relate it to the rest of the lecture information.

- When you respond, include **transition words** where they are appropriate. Doing so will make one idea flow smoothly into the next. See below for a sample of a completed response.

| | Notes | Response |
|---|---|---|
| **Lecture Main Idea** | determine if a thing can be proven true | The lecture talks about the importance of knowing whether a statement can be proven true or not. |
| **Summary of Subtopic 1** | obj. statement = provable<br><br>ex. insect eaters | According to the lecture, if a statement is provable, it's said to be objective. The lecture uses the statement that many people eat insects as an example of an objective statement. Because a survey could prove that this statement is true or false, it must be objective. |
| **Summary of Subtopic 2** | subj. statement = opinion<br><br>ex. bugs delicious/ disgusting | **Conversely**, according to the lecture, opinions are subjective. They can't be proven using any test or experiment. **For example**, "eating bugs is disgusting" is a subjective claim because someone else could say the opposite. So, neither opinion will ever be objectively correct. |

 Review the following lecture and prompt. Then write a Task 6 response. Review your notes from the previous practices if necessary. Once you have written down your response, **say it aloud to yourself, a friend, a classmate, or a family member**.

### LECTURE

**Animal Migration**

*Each year, thousands of animal species travel from one region to another in a process known as "migration." Almost all animals migrate to find food, a better climate, or a place to breed.*

*Let's take a look at the migration of humpback whales. During the summer, humpback whales search for food in the cold, nutrient-rich waters near the north and south poles. But these waters are too cold for breeding, so during the winter months, the whales travel to the warmer waters near the equator to breed. This roundtrip journey can total about 25,000 kilometers.*

*Pacific salmon also undergo a difficult migration. After reaching adulthood in the ocean, the salmon will travel to freshwater rivers, where they swim upstream so they can breed in the same places they were born. The few salmon that survive the difficult journey die after breeding.*

### Prompt

Using examples from the lecture, explain some of the reasons that animals migrate.

### Response

_____
_____
_____
_____
_____
_____
_____
_____
_____

# EXERCISE 1

Following the steps below, develop a response to the following prompt.

## STEP 1. OUTLINE YOUR RESPONSE

**LECTURE**

### Advertising Strategies

Nowadays, advertisements are everywhere; nearly every website is covered in ads, and even some of the clothing we wear contains some sort of logo. Today I want to talk about two ways that advertisers convince the public to buy their products.

One way that advertisers sell products is by appealing to an audience's pathos, or emotions. For example, a television commercial for an amusement park may show laughing children, or people smiling as they ride roller coasters, causing the viewer to relate the amusement park to happiness.

A second advertising technique involves appealing to logos, or an audience's desire for facts and logic. For instance, a snack food might advertise that it contains 75 percent less fat than other similar snack foods. Here the use of certain statistics makes the product seem healthy and therefore appealing.

**LECTURE NOTES**

Main Idea: _____

- Subtopic 1: _____

    Details: _____

    _____

- Subtopic 2: _____

    Details: _____

    _____

**Prompt**

Using specific details and examples from the lecture, explain how the two advertising strategies discussed in the lecture influence consumers.

## STEP 2. PREPARE YOUR RESPONSE          00:00:20

1) Summarize the main idea of the lecture.

   **From Notes** → Main Idea: _____

2) Explain the first subtopic presented in the lecture.

   **From Notes** → Subtopic 1: _____
   
   _____

3) Explain the second subtopic presented in the lecture.

   **From Notes** → Subtopic 2: _____
   
   _____

## STEP 3. DELIVER YOUR RESPONSE          00:01:00

**Response**

_____
_____
_____
_____
_____
_____
_____
_____

# EXERCISE 1
*Evaluation*

**Now practice saying your response aloud.** If possible, have a friend/classmate fill out this checklist as you say your response to him or her. If you are by yourself, record and listen to your response, and then fill out the checklist below on your own.

Deliver your response within 60 seconds.

## Task 6 Response Checklist

| | Yes | Somewhat | No |
|---|---|---|---|
| • Does the speaker briefly describe the main concept of the lecture? | | | |
| • Does the speaker summarize the two examples/topics that elaborate on the lecture's main concepts? | | | |
| • Does the speaker explain how these two examples/topics relate to one another? | | | |
| • Does the speaker deliver an organized response by using transition words and proper sentence structures? | | | |
| • Does the speaker deliver a coherent response by using appropriate tone and pronunciation? | | | |
| • Does the speaker finish within the time limit? | | ✗ | |

*Model Answer*

---

**LECTURE NOTES**

**Main Idea:** how ads work (ad strategies)

- **Subtopic 1:** appeal to emotions
    - **Details:** ex: amusement park → happy people
- **Subtopic 2:** appeal to logic/facts
    - **Details:** ex: use stats. (food w/ ↓ fat)

---

1) Summarize the main idea of the lecture.

   **From Notes → Main Idea:** how ads work (ad strategies)

2) Explain the first subtopic presented in the lecture.

   **From Notes → Subtopic 1:** appeal to emotions

   amusement park ad shows happy ppl. → connect park w/ happiness

3) Explain the second subtopic presented in the lecture.

   **From Notes → Subtopic 2:** appeal to logic/facts

   stats in ads, snack food ads claim reduced fat

 **Response**

The lecture discusses two types of advertising strategies. The first strategy the professor talks about involves appealing to a person's emotions. For instance, the lecture describes an ad for an amusement park that shows people having fun while riding roller coasters. When people see this ad, they'll expect that if they went to the amusement park, they'd also be happy. The second strategy involves giving logical reasons that a person should buy a product. For example, some snack foods advertise that they have less fat than other snacks. This is supposed to make them seem healthy and therefore desirable.

# EXERCISE 2

Following the steps below, develop a response to the following prompt.

## STEP 1. OUTLINE YOUR RESPONSE

**LECTURE**

### Diets

People diet for many reasons. Some diet to become healthier while others choose to diet for moral reasons. Two of the most popular diets are vegetarian and veganism. Although these diets have many similarities, there are also some important differences between the two.

Vegetarians don't eat meat, but many vegetarians will still consume animal products such as milk, cheese, and eggs. However, some vegetarians choose to avoid certain animal products but still use others, so they might, for example, avoid eggs but consume dairy products.

Veganism is a type of vegetarianism, but vegans generally believe that raising animals just to use them for their meat, milk, or skin is cruel. Therefore, vegans don't eat any animal products, including dairy and eggs. Moreover, many vegans don't wear leather and sometimes even avoid wearing wool, as these products come from the skin and fur of livestock.

**LECTURE NOTES**

Main Idea: _____

- Subtopic 1: _____

    Details: _____

    _____

- Subtopic 2: _____

    Details: _____

    _____

**Prompt**

Using details and examples from the lecture, explain the similarities and differences between vegetarianism and veganism.

## STEP 2. PREPARE YOUR RESPONSE  00:00:20

1) Summarize the main idea of the lecture.

   **From Notes** → Main Idea: _____

2) Explain the first subtopic presented in the lecture.

   **From Notes** → Subtopic 1: _____
   
   _____

3) Explain the second subtopic presented in the lecture.

   **From Notes** → Subtopic 2: _____
   
   _____

## STEP 3. DELIVER YOUR RESPONSE  00:01:00

**Response**

_____
_____
_____
_____
_____
_____
_____
_____

# EXERCISE 2     *Evaluation*

**Now practice saying your response aloud.** If possible, have a friend/classmate fill out this checklist as you say your response to him or her. If you are by yourself, record and listen to your response, and then fill out the checklist below on your own.

Deliver your response within 60 seconds.

## Task 6 Response Checklist

|  | Yes | Somewhat | No |
|---|---|---|---|
| • Does the speaker briefly describe the main concept of the lecture? | | | |
| • Does the speaker summarize the two examples/topics that elaborate on the lecture's main concepts? | | | |
| • Does the speaker explain how these two examples/topics relate to one another? | | | |
| • Does the speaker deliver an organized response by using transition words and proper sentence structures? | | | |
| • Does the speaker deliver a coherent response by using appropriate tone and pronunciation? | | | |
| • Does the speaker finish within the time limit? | | ✗ | |

*Model Answer*

### LECTURE NOTES

**Main Idea:** type of diet

- **Subtopic 1:** vegetarian diets

    **Details:** no meat but anim. products usually OK (milk, cheese)

- **Subtopic 2:** vegan diet

    **Details:** no meat, no anim. products → morally wrong to eat/wear (milk, leather)

1) Summarize the main idea of the lecture.

    **From Notes → Main Idea:** type of diet (vegetarian and vegan)

2) Explain the first subtopic presented in the lecture.

    **From Notes → Subtopic 1:** vegetarian diet

    no meat but animal products usually OK (milk, cheese)

3) Explain the second subtopic presented in the lecture.

    **From Notes → Subtopic 2:** vegan diet

    no meat, no animal products → morally wrong to eat/wear (milk, leather)

 **Response**

The lecture discusses two types of diets: vegetarianism and veganism. Vegetarians don't eat meat, but many vegetarians will consume food that comes from animals, such as milk or cheese. Like vegetarians, vegans avoid eating meat, but vegans don't use any animal products at all. Thus, vegans don't eat food that comes from animals, and they don't wear clothing made from animals, such as wool or leather. According to the lecture, vegans avoid all animal products because they believe that animal exploitation is morally wrong.

# EXERCISE 3

Following the steps below, develop a response to the following prompt.

## STEP 1. OUTLINE YOUR RESPONSE

**LECTURE**

**Poetry and Prose**

People have been keeping written records for about 6,000 years, the earliest of these being marks in clay slabs. So today, I'd like to talk about the two most basic styles of writing that have existed since ancient times: poetry and prose.

Generally poetry consists of words selected and arranged to make the reader "see" an image, feel an emotion, or learn a story. Poetry, whether spoken or sung, usually has some kind of rhythm. As a result, even before writing, people preserved information in the form of poems, because poetry is easier to memorize.

In contrast, most writing today is in prose, such as articles, novels, and text messages. Prose is "ordinary" in the sense that it sounds like speech. Prose writing mimics the natural pauses and tones of spoken language.

**LECTURE NOTES**

Main Idea: _____

- Subtopic 1: _____

    Details: _____
    _____

- Subtopic 2: _____

    Details: _____
    _____

**Prompt**

Using specific details from the lecture, explain the qualities and functions of poetry and prose.

## STEP 2. PREPARE YOUR RESPONSE  00:00:20

1) Summarize the main idea of the lecture.

   **From Notes** → Main Idea: _____

2) Explain the first subtopic presented in the lecture.

   **From Notes** → Subtopic 1: _____
   
   _____

3) Explain the second subtopic presented in the lecture.

   **From Notes** → Subtopic 2: _____
   
   _____

## STEP 3. DELIVER YOUR RESPONSE  00:01:00

**Response**

_____
_____
_____
_____
_____
_____
_____
_____
_____

# EXERCISE 3  *Evaluation*

**Now practice saying your response aloud.** If possible, have a friend/classmate fill out this checklist as you say your response to him or her. If you are by yourself, record and listen to your response, and then fill out the checklist below on your own.

Deliver your response within 60 seconds.

## Task 6 Response Checklist

|  | Yes | Somewhat | No |
|---|---|---|---|
| • Does the speaker briefly describe the main concept of the lecture? | | | |
| • Does the speaker summarize the two examples/topics that elaborate on the lecture's main concepts? | | | |
| • Does the speaker explain how these two examples/topics relate to one another? | | | |
| • Does the speaker deliver an organized response by using transition words and proper sentence structures? | | | |
| • Does the speaker deliver a coherent response by using appropriate tone and pronunciation? | | | |
| • Does the speaker finish within the time limit? | | ✗ | |

# Model Answer

## LECTURE NOTES

**Main Idea:** two types of writing → poetry & prose

- **Subtopic 1:** poetry → word arrangement important
  - **Details:** rhythm → easier to memorize; used before writing
- **Subtopic 2:** prose → most writing nowadays
  - **Details:** like spoken lang.

1) Summarize the main idea of the lecture.

   **From Notes → Main Idea:** two types of writing → poetry and prose

2) Explain the first subtopic presented in the lecture.

   **From Notes → Subtopic 1:** poetry → word arrangement important

   uses rhythm → easier to memorize; used before writing developed

3) Explain the second subtopic presented in the lecture.

   **From Notes → Subtopic 2:** prose → most writing nowadays

   like spoken language

### Response

The lecture discusses the two most basic ways that people have expressed ideas through writing for thousands of years. The first style discussed is poetry. In poetry, words are chosen and placed carefully to get the reader to picture or feel certain things. Because poetry usually has a certain rhythm, it's often easier to memorize, so people have long used poetry in order to pass on information. On the other hand, prose is more like natural speech, written in such a way to sound like it's being spoken. Prose is the style used for most of the writing we see in current times.

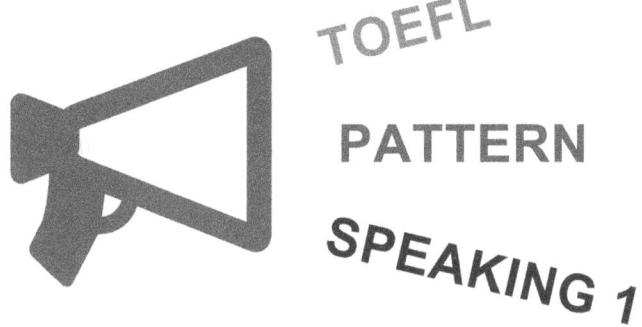

# CHAPTER 7

# Actual Practice

# TOEFL iBT Independent Speaking Task Rubric (Tasks 1-2)

## 4

**OVERVIEW**
- *Although the response may include brief lapses\* in clarity, the vast majority of the response is intelligible and comprehensive. For a response to receive a score of 4, it must accomplish all of the following:*

**SPEECH**
- The speaker delivers an articulate response that requires little to no interpretation on the part of the listener. Any mistakes or omissions do not affect the listener's ability to comprehend the speaker's response.

**VOCABULARY AND GRAMMAR**
- The speaker demonstrates his or her command of a sophisticated vocabulary and an understanding of various sentence structures. Minimal pauses indicate a strong familiarity with the English language. Any vocabulary or grammar mistakes do not affect the listener's ability to understand the response.

**CONTENT**
- The speaker completely addresses all aspects of the prompt by presenting ideas in a logical and organized manner.

## 3

**OVERVIEW**
- *The response may contain noticeable lapses in clarity and organization, but it is still consistently intelligible and exhibits a clear understanding of the prompt. for a response to receive a score of 3, it must accomplish at least two of the following:*

**SPEECH**
- The speaker delivers a response that is generally comprehensible, but noticeable pronunciation or inflection issues may occasionally obscure the speaker's meaning.

**VOCABULARY AND GRAMMAR**
- Although the speaker's grasp of vocabulary and grammar structures may be somewhat limited and occasionally inaccurate, any errors or mistakes do not greatly interfere with the speaker's overall ability to respond to the prompt.

**CONTENT**
- The speaker addresses all aspects of the prompt, even though the response may lack detailed explanations and may contain lapses in organization.

\***Lapse**: a temporary decline in quality of something

## 2

**OVERVIEW**
- *The response includes information relevant to the prompt, but the listener's comprehension is hindered by frequent lapses in the speaker's fluency. For a response to receive a score of 2, it must accomplish at least two of the following:*

**SPEECH**
- The speaker delivers a response that requires active interpretation on the part of the listener. Although most of the response is intelligible, frequent pronunciation and inflection issues obscure the speaker's meaning.

**VOCABULARY AND GRAMMAR**
- A limited grasp of vocabulary and grammar structures often prevents the speaker from fully articulating his or her thoughts. The response is dominated by short, simple sentences and is characterized by a limited vocabulary.

**CONTENT**
- The response generally connects to the prompt, but it lacks details and examples. The few details and examples that are presented may be unclear or redundant.

## 1

**OVERVIEW**
- *The response barely addresses the prompt, and/or the majority of the response is incomprehensible. For a response to receive a score of 1, it must accomplish at least two of the following:*

**SPEECH**
- Frequent and reoccurring pronunciation and inflection issues make most of the response difficult to understand, if not entirely incomprehensible. Constant interpretation is required on the part of the listener.

**VOCABULARY AND GRAMMAR**
- A limited grasp of vocabulary and grammar prevents the speaker from articulating his or her thoughts. The speaker may rely heavily on clichés or memorized phrases and expressions.

**CONTENT**
- The speaker conveys little information that is relevant to the prompt. Only simple ideas are presented, and these ideas may be unclear or redundant.

## 0

**OVERVIEW**
- *The speaker does not respond to the prompt. The speaker may deliver a response that is unrelated to the prompt, or the speaker may deliver a response in a language other than English.*

# TOEFL iBT Integrated Speaking Task Rubric (Tasks 3-6)

| | |
|---|---|
| **4** | **OVERVIEW**<br>- *The speaker addresses all aspects of the prompt. Despite infrequent lapses in clarity, the response is intelligible and comprehensive. For a response to a receive a score of 4, it must address all of the following:*<br><br>**SPEECH**<br>- The speaker may pause in order to recall or reference information, but these pauses do not affect the listener's comprehension. Similarly, any mistakes or omissions do not affect the listener's ability to comprehend the speaker's response.<br><br>**VOCABULARY AND GRAMMAR**<br>- The speaker demonstrates his or her command of a sophisticated vocabulary and an understanding of various sentence structures. Minimal pauses indicate a strong familiarity with the English language. Any vocabulary or grammar mistakes do not affect the listener's ability to understand the response. The speaker uses nearly all relevant terms from the listening and/or reading portions of the task.<br><br>**CONTENT**<br>- The speaker organizes and presents nearly all relevant information presented in the task. The relationships between ideas are consistently clear. |
| **3** | **OVERVIEW**<br>- *The response may contain noticeable lapses in clarity and organization, but it is still consistently intelligible and exhibits a clear understanding of the requirements of the task. For a response to receive a score of 3, it must accomplish at least two of the following:*<br><br>**SPEECH**<br>- The speaker delivers a response that is generally comprehensible, but noticeable pronunciation or inflection issues may occasionally interfere with the speaker's ability to convey information presented in the task.<br><br>**VOCABULARY AND GRAMMAR**<br>- Although the speaker's grasp of vocabulary and grammar structures may be somewhat limited and occasionally inaccurate, any errors or mistakes do not greatly interfere with the speaker's overall ability to form a response. The speaker uses some relevant terms from the listening and/or reading portions of the task.<br><br>**CONTENT**<br>- The speaker addresses most of the relevant information presented in the task, but the response may be missing some details, contain some inaccurate information, or include lapses in organization and clarity. |

## 2

### OVERVIEW
- *The response includes information relevant to the task, but some information may be inaccurate or omitted altogether. A lack of clarity or intelligibility may interfere with the listener's comprehension of the response. For a response to receive a score of 2, it must accomplish at least two of the following:*

### SPEECH
- The speaker delivers a response that requires active interpretation on the part of the listener. Although most of the response is intelligible, frequent pronunciation and inflection issues obscure the speaker's meaning.

### VOCABULARY AND GRAMMAR
- A limited grasp of vocabulary and grammar structures often prevent the speaker from fully articulating his or her thoughts. The response is dominated by short, simple sentences and is characterized by a limited vocabulary. The speaker uses few relevant terms from the listening and/or reading portions of the task.

### CONTENT
- The response relates to the information presented in the task, but it contains many obvious omissions or inaccuracies. Any main ideas are explained vaguely or inaccurately, and main ideas may be confused with minor details or irrelevant information presented in the listening and/or reading portions of the task.

## 1

### OVERVIEW
- *The response includes very few pieces of information that are relevant to the task, and/or the majority of the response is incomprehensible. For a response to receive a score of 1, it must accomplish at least two of the following:*

### SPEECH
- Frequent and reoccurring pronunciation and inflection issues make most of the response difficult to understand, if not entirely incomprehensible. Constant interpretation is required on the part of the listener.

### VOCABULARY AND GRAMMAR
- A limited grasp of vocabulary and grammar prevents the speaker from articulating his or her thoughts. The speaker may rely heavily on clichés or memorized phrases and expressions. The speaker does not use any relevant terms from the listening and/or reading portions of the task.

### CONTENT
- The speaker conveys little information that is relevant to the information presented in the task. Only simple ideas are presented, and these ideas may be unclear or redundant.

## 0

### OVERVIEW
- *The speaker does not respond to the prompt. The speaker may deliver a response that is unrelated to the prompt, or the speaker may deliver a response in a language other than English.*

# Task 1

**Prompt**

Describe a person who has inspired you. Explain what qualities make this person inspirational. Use specific reasons and details to support your answer.

 Preparation Time 00:00:15
Response Time 00:00:45

**Notes**

The person who has inspired me is _____.

- _____
- _____

**Response**

_____
_____
_____
_____
_____
_____
_____
_____
_____
_____
_____

# Task 2

> **Prompt**
> Some people prefer to take extra classes while attending a university, which allows them to earn a degree quickly. Other people like to take an average class load each quarter or semester. Which do you prefer? Use specific reasons and details to support your answer.

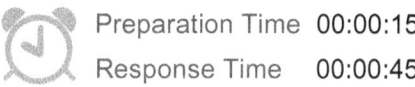

Preparation Time 00:00:15
Response Time 00:00:45

## Notes

I prefer to take (**extra classes / an average class load**) each quarter or semester.

- _____
- _____

## Response

_____
_____
_____
_____
_____
_____
_____
_____
_____

ACTUAL PRACTICE ♦ CHAPTER 7

# Task 1

## Model Answer

**Prompt**

Describe a person who has inspired you. Explain what qualities make this person inspirational. Use specific reasons and details to support your answer.

### Notes

The person who has inspired me is ___Mohandas Gandhi___.

- _nonviolence → independence to India_
- _leader for social reform → rights for women & poor (untouch.)_

 **Response**

Mohandas Gandhi, also known as Mahatma Gandhi, is an inspiring person to me. There are several reasons why. For one, he overcame obstacles using nonviolence. His nonviolent protests helped lead India to independence from Great Britain. Another reason I admire him is that he was a leader for social reform. He supported the rights of women and of the poorest people, who were called the "untouchables."

# TASK 2

### Model Answer

**Prompt**

Some people prefer to take extra classes while attending a university, which allows them to earn a degree quickly. Other people like to take an average class load each quarter or semester. Which do you prefer? Use specific reasons and details to support your answer.

**Notes**

I prefer to take (**extra classes** / *an average class load*) each quarter or semester.

- *more time to absorb material → understand material better*
- *don't like feeling rushed → no pressure*

 **Response**

Some people choose to take more classes to graduate sooner, but I prefer to take an average load each quarter. One reason is that I need time to absorb what I learn in my classes. I want to be sure I understand everything I learn. Another reason is that I don't like feeling rushed. I perform better when I'm not under pressure. For these reasons, I enjoy having a normal amount of assignments and tests each quarter or semester.

# Task 3

**ACTUAL PRACTICE 1**

## UNIVERSITY ANNOUNCEMENT

### New Vegetable Garden

The university will be starting a vegetable garden near the east end of campus next semester. The vegetables grown will be used in the student dining hall. The dining hall's staff will recycle leftover food from the kitchen for composting. The compost will be used to improve the quality of the soil that is used to grow organic produce.

### Announcement Notes

Proposal: _____

* _____

* _____

## CONVERSATION

**F:** I think starting an on-campus garden is a great idea. What do you think?

**M:** I think so, too!

**F:** The garden will help the school in so many ways. For one, it'll lower school expenses.

**M:** How will it do that?

**F:** Well, putting the leftover food from the kitchen in the garden reduces garbage pick-up costs for the school. Plus the school will save money by growing vegetables rather than buying them.

**M:** You know, that's a really good point.

**F:** Another reason I like this garden idea is that we'll end up with fresh, organic food in our on-campus dining hall.

*F: Female Student / M: Male Student*

### Conversation Notes

Speaker's opinion: _____

* _____

* _____

> **Prompt**
>
> The woman expresses her opinion about the plan described in the announcement. Briefly summarize the plan. Then state her opinion about the plan and explain her reasons for holding that opinion.

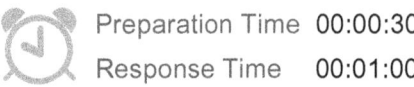

Preparation Time  00:00:30
Response Time    00:01:00

Use your 30 seconds of "Preparation Time" to organize your notes and prepare for your response.

Write your response on the lines below. Then **say your response aloud**, making sure that you can deliver your response in 1 minute.

### Response

___
___
___
___
___
___
___
___
___

# Task 4

### PASSAGE

**Sacajawea**

Sacajawea was a Native American of the Shoshone tribes. In 1805, when she was just 16 years old, she and her husband served as guides for the Lewis and Clark Expedition. The expedition was exploring territories that the United States had recently purchased from France. Carrying her newborn son, Sacajawea traveled with the explorers across the Rocky Mountains and to the Pacific Ocean and back.

**Passage Notes**

Main Idea: _____

· _____

· _____

### LECTURE

Without Sacajawea, the Lewis and Clark Expedition might've failed, and many members of the expedition likely would've died.

For example, Sacajawea's familiarity with the native plants and animals of the American West helped provide food for the expedition. She prevented starvation by finding food, such as roots and plants, for the members of the expedition to eat.

Furthermore, she knew the culture and sometimes even the language of other Native American tribes. Because of this, she was able to help the expedition trade their supplies for horses and other goods. Sacajawea's presence also reassured Native American tribes that the expedition was peaceful.

**Lecture Notes**

Topic: _____

Example 1: _____

· Details: _____

Example 2: _____

· Details: _____

> **Prompt**
> Explain how the examples from the lecture illustrate the ways in which Sacajawea helped the Lewis and Clark Expedition.

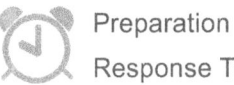
Preparation Time 00:00:30
Response Time 00:01:00

Use your 30 seconds of "Preparation Time" to organize your notes and prepare for your response.

Write your response on the lines below. Then **say your response aloud**, making sure that you can deliver your response in 1 minute.

**Response**

___
___
___
___
___
___
___
___
___

# TASK 3

## Model Answer

### UNIVERSITY ANNOUNCEMENT

**New Vegetable Garden**

The university will be starting a vegetable garden near the east end of campus next semester. The vegetables grown will be used in the student dining hall. The dining hall's staff will recycle leftover food from the kitchen for composting. The compost will be used to improve the quality of the soil that is used to grow organic produce.

### CONVERSATION

**F:** I think starting an on-campus garden is a great idea. What do you think?
**M:** I think so, too!
**F:** The garden will help the school in so many ways. For one, it'll lower school expenses.
**M:** How will it do that?
**F:** Well, putting the leftover food from the kitchen in the garden reduces garbage pick-up costs for the school. Plus the school will save money by growing vegetables rather than buying them.
**M:** You know, that's a really good point.
**F:** Another reason I like this garden idea is that we'll end up with fresh, organic food in our on-campus dining hall.

### Prompt

The woman expresses her opinion about the plan described in the announcement. Briefly summarize the plan. Then state her opinion about the plan and explain her reasons for holding that opinion.

**Announcement Notes**

Proposal: _start campus garden_

- vege. garden → dining hall
- leftover food → compost

**Conversation Notes**

Speaker's opinion: _woman supports_

- save $ → ↓ garbage/vege. costs
- get organic food in dining hall

### Response

The university plans to start a garden and recycle leftover food from the school's kitchen for compost. Vegetables will go to the student dining hall. The woman supports the plan. One reason is that the garden will reduce garbage removal and food costs, so it could save the school money and help the environment. She also likes the plan because the dining hall will offer fresh organic vegetables.

# TASK 4

## Model Answer

### PASSAGE

**Sacajawea**

Sacajawea was a Native American of the Shoshone tribes. In 1805, when she was just 16 years old, she and her husband served as guides for the Lewis and Clark Expedition. The expedition was exploring territories that the United States had recently purchased from France. Carrying her newborn son, Sacajawea traveled with the explorers across the Rocky Mountains and to the Pacific Ocean and back.

### LECTURE

Without Sacajawea, the Lewis and Clark Expedition might've failed, and many members of the expedition likely would've died.

For example, Sacajawea's familiarity with the native plants and animals of the American West helped provide food for the expedition. She prevented starvation by finding food, such as roots and plants, for the members of the expedition to eat.

Furthermore, she knew the culture and sometimes even the language of other Native American tribes. Because of this, she was able to help the expedition trade their supplies for horses and other goods. Sacajawea's presence also reassured Native American tribes that the expedition was peaceful.

### Prompt

Explain how the examples from the lecture illustrate the ways in which Sacajawea helped the Lewis and Clark Expedition.

**Passage Notes**

Main Idea: *SJ → helped L & C (1805)*

- *explored new territories*
- *carried baby there & back*

**Lecture Notes**

Topic: *SJ crucial to L & C*

Example 1: *SJ found food*

- Details: *fam. w/ plant/animal of region*

Example 2: *SJ avoided conflict*

- Details: *helped trade w/ Nat. Am.*

 **Response**

The reading explains that Sacajawea, a Native American, helped the Lewis and Clark expedition explore new U.S. territories in 1805. The lecture points out that she helped the group survive. For example, she knew how to find food for the members of the expedition because she was familiar with the area. She also helped the group avoid conflict with Native American tribes and trade with some of the tribes the expedition encountered.

# Task 5

## ACTUAL PRACTICE 1

### CONVERSATION

**M:** Hey, Mary, I need some advice. I can't decide on the topic for my paper.

**F:** Maybe I can help you. What class is the paper for?

**M:** Chinese history, and I'm not even certain what era to focus on.

**F:** Have you talked to the instructor? I took that class last year, and the professor was really helpful when I asked her to help me with my writing difficulties. Her advice helped me get an "A" in the class.

**M:** That might be a good idea. Maybe she can suggest a starting point for my research.

**F:** Another thought is that you might want to do a little research to see what interests you. After all, you'll never be able to decide on a topic until you know a little bit more about the subject.

**M:** I see your point, but I'm so busy with my other classes that it's hard to find time for research.

**M:** Male Student / **F:** Female Student

---

### Conversation Notes

Speaker's problem: _____

- Solution 1: _____

- Solution 2: _____

> **Prompt**
> Briefly summarize the problem the speakers are discussing. Then state which of the two solutions from the conversation you would recommend. Explain the reasons for your recommendation.

Preparation Time  00:00:20
Response Time    00:01:00

Use your 20 seconds of "Preparation Time" to organize your notes and prepare for your response.

### Preparation Notes

Preferred solution: _____

- Reason 1: _____

- Reason 2: _____

Write your response on the lines below. Then **say your response aloud**, making sure that you can deliver your response in 1 minute.

### 📣 Response

_____
_____
_____
_____
_____
_____
_____
_____
_____

# TASK 6

## LECTURE

### Primates

*Primates are a diverse order of mammals that mostly inhabit tropical, forested regions. The first primates were small, tree-dwelling creatures that appeared about 55 million years ago. Most primates can be classified as either apes or monkeys.*

*Apes are tailless, and they use their long, powerful arms for climbing. Moreover, apes are generally larger and have bigger brains than monkeys. Consequently, some species of ape use their large brains to create tools, such as sharpened sticks, to help them get food. Examples of apes include chimpanzees and gorillas.*

*Monkeys have long, flexible tails that they use when climbing trees. They crawl along branches and use their long legs to leap from tree to tree. Some species of monkeys are the tree-dwelling squirrel monkey and the ground-dwelling baboon.*

### Lecture Notes

Main Idea: _____

Subtopic 1: _____

- Details: _____

_____

Subtopic 2: _____

- Details: _____

_____

> **Prompt**
> Using examples from the lecture, explain some similarities and differences between apes and monkeys.

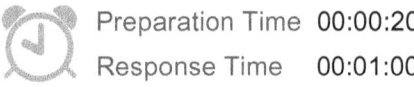
Preparation Time 00:00:20
Response Time 00:01:00

Use your 20 seconds of "Preparation Time" to organize your notes and prepare for your response.

Write your response on the lines below. Then **say your response aloud**, making sure that you can deliver your response in 1 minute.

### Response

_____
_____
_____
_____
_____
_____
_____
_____
_____

# Task 5

## Model Answer

### CONVERSATION

**M:** Hey, Mary, I need some advice. I can't decide on the topic for my paper.
**F:** Maybe I can help you. What class is the paper for?
**M:** Chinese history, and I'm not even certain what era to focus on.
**F:** Have you talked to the instructor? I took that class last year, and the professor was really helpful when I asked her to help me with my writing difficulties. Her advice helped me get an "A" in the class.
**M:** That might be a good idea. Maybe she can suggest a starting point for my research.
**F:** Another thought is that you might want to do a little research to see what interests you. After all, you'll never be able to decide on a topic until you know a little bit more about the subject.
**M:** I see your point, but I'm so busy with my other classes that it's hard to find time for research.

### Prompt

Briefly summarize the problem the speakers are discussing. Then state which of the two solutions from the conversation you would recommend. Explain the reasons for your recommendation.

### Conversation Notes

Speaker's problem: *man doesn't have a topic for his paper*

- Solution 1: *talk to prof.*
- Solution 2: *research first*

### Preparation Notes

Preferred solution: *research first*

- Reason 1: *might find topic*
- Reason 2: *make some effort before going to prof.*

### Response

The problem is that the man can't decide on a topic for his paper. The woman suggests that he either talk to his instructor or do some research. Personally, I think he should first do the research. One reason is that he might find a topic he likes. Another reason is that he at least needs to try to figure out a solution to the issue before approaching the instructor.

# Task 6

## Model Answer

### LECTURE

**Primates**

Primates are a diverse order of mammals that mostly inhabit tropical, forested regions. The first primates were small, tree-dwelling creatures that appeared about 55 million years ago. Most primates can be classified as either apes or monkeys.

Apes are tailless, and they use their long, powerful arms for climbing. Moreover, apes are generally larger and have bigger brains than monkeys. Consequently, some species of ape use their large brains to create tools, such as sharpened sticks, to help them get food. Examples of apes include chimpanzees and gorillas.

Monkeys have long, flexible tails that they use when climbing trees. They crawl along branches and use their long legs to leap from tree to tree. Some species of monkeys are the tree-dwelling squirrel monkey and the ground-dwelling baboon.

### Prompt

Using examples from the lecture, explain some similarities and differences between apes and monkeys.

### Lecture Notes

Main Idea: *primates → mammals, live in tropic forests*

Subtopic 1: *apes*

- Details: *no tail, large, strong arms; big brains → tool use*

    *ex. chimp & gorilla*

Subtopic 2: *monkeys*

- Details: *long tail, long legs (tree climbing)*

    *ex. squirrel monkey & baboon*

### Response

The professor describes some qualities of apes and monkeys. Both are primates, which are mammals that usually live in tropical forests. Apes have long arms and no tails, whereas monkeys have long tails and long legs that they use for climbing trees. Moreover, apes are large, big-brained mammals that sometimes use tools for gathering food. According to the lecture, monkeys are usually smaller than apes. Some examples of apes are chimpanzees and gorillas, and some monkeys include squirrel monkeys and baboons.

# Task 1

**Prompt**

What are the most important qualities for a friend to possess? Use specific details in your explanation.

Preparation Time 00:00:15
Response Time 00:00:45

**Notes**

Important qualities for a friend: _____

" _____

" _____

**Response**

_____
_____
_____
_____
_____
_____
_____
_____
_____
_____

# TASK 2

**Prompt**

Do you agree or disagree with the following statement? It is more important to take classes that provide information about the latest technology than to enroll in art or creative writing courses. Why or why not? Use details and examples to explain your answer.

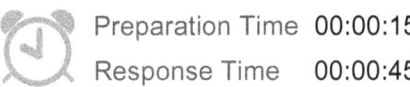

Preparation Time  00:00:15
Response Time    00:00:45

**Notes**

I **(agree / disagree)**.

* _____
* _____

**Response**

# Task 1

## Model Answer

**Prompt**

What are the most important qualities for a friend to possess? Use specific details in your explanation.

### Notes

Important qualities for a friend: _similar interests, humor_

- similar interests → ex. running w/ friend

- sense of humor → cheer me up, problems ↓

 **Response**

Two important characteristics of a close friend are similar interests to my own and a good sense of humor. For instance, my best friend and I both love to run, so we go running together every weekend. On these runs, we talk about any problems in our lives. And by the end of the run, my problems are always less troublesome because my friend is able to put things into perspective using her sharp sense of humor.

# TASK 2

## Model Answer

**Prompt**

Do you agree or disagree with the following statement? It is more important to take classes that provide information about the latest technology than to enroll in art or creative writing courses. Why or why not? Use details and examples to explain your answer.

### Notes

I (**agree** / *<u>disagree</u>*).

- *diff. interests → prefer creativity, bad w/ comps.*
- *salary → not everything*

 **Response**

I disagree with the statement, primarily because I'm not very interested in technology. Dealing with computers has always brought me more frustration than satisfaction. So I'd rather take a class that encourages imagination and creativity, such as painting or writing. And even though working in a field such as computer programming may mean earning a larger salary than working as a writer or critic, money is not the only thing that brings a person satisfaction.

# Task 3

**UNIVERSITY ANNOUNCEMENT**

### University to Change Course Length

The university is proposing having two semesters a year instead of three quarters. Students would take five classes at a time instead of three classes, but daily class periods would be shorter. A recent study shows that students gain more knowledge when coursework is spread out over time. Furthermore, the semester system would reduce administrative costs for the school.

### Announcement Notes

Proposal: _____

_____

_____

**CONVERSATION**

**M:** Ugh, I'm not happy about the university's proposal.

**F:** Tell me about it.

**M:** I want to finish the required classes faster. I don't want to spend half my school year in a class that I really have no interest in.

**F:** Yeah, me neither!

**M:** And anyway, I just don't like the slower pace of the semester system.

**F:** I'm with you on that.

**M:** I like taking more classes in a shorter time. I feel like I learn more when I'm presented with such a wide variety of information. I know I'll just get bored if I'm forced to take a class for a whole semester.

*M: Male Student / F: Female Student*

### Conversation Notes

Speaker's opinion: _____

_____

_____

> **Prompt**
>
> The man expresses his opinion about the announcement described in the article. Briefly summarize the proposal. Then state his opinion about the announcement and explain the reasons he gives for holding that opinion.

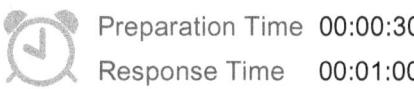

Preparation Time  00:00:30
Response Time     00:01:00

Use your 30 seconds of "Preparation Time" to organize your notes and prepare for your response.

Write your response on the lines below. Then **say your response aloud**, making sure that you can deliver your response in 1 minute.

**Response**

_____
_____
_____
_____
_____
_____
_____
_____
_____

# Task 4

## PASSAGE

### Teen Obesity in the United States

Over the past three decades, the number of obese children in the United States has more than doubled. These obesity rates are even higher among children from poor families. However, there are a number of ways that communities can work together to help reduce the alarmingly high rates of childhood obesity in the U.S.

### Passage Notes

Main Idea: _____

_____

_____

## LECTURE

Today I'd like to talk about two consequences of the teen obesity problem in the U.S. These consequences are so severe that Americans need to spend time and money trying to prevent teen obesity through projects such as building more parks in poor neighborhoods.

The worst consequence of teen obesity is an increased risk for disease from a young age. People who are obese are more likely to develop a number of serious health conditions, including heart disease, diabetes, stroke, and cancer. Communities should try to prevent these serious health problems for their citizens and workforce by educating young people about the health risks associated with obesity.

Another reason that communities must work to reduce teen obesity is that the treatment of obesity-related diseases is expensive. Some experts estimate that treating obesity-related diseases in the U.S. costs nearly 200 billion dollars per year. The result is higher insurance costs and higher taxes for everyone.

### Lecture Notes

Topic: _____

Example 1: _____

- Details: _____

Example 2: _____

- Details: _____

> **Prompt**
> Using the professor's examples, explain two consequences of teen obesity in the United States.

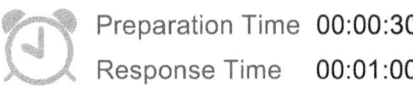

Preparation Time 00:00:30
Response Time 00:01:00

Use your 30 seconds of "Preparation Time" to organize your notes and prepare for your response.

Write your response on the lines below. Then **say your response aloud**, making sure that you can deliver your response in 1 minute.

### Response

_____
_____
_____
_____
_____
_____
_____
_____
_____
_____

# Task 3

## Model Answer

### UNIVERSITY ANNOUNCEMENT

**University to Change Course Length**

The university is proposing having two semesters a year instead of three quarters. Students would take five classes at a time instead of three classes, but daily class periods would be shorter. A recent study shows that students gain more knowledge when coursework is spread out over time. Furthermore, the semester system would reduce administrative costs for the school.

### CONVERSATION

**M:** Ugh, I'm not happy about the university's proposal.
**F:** Tell me about it.
**M:** I want to finish the required classes faster. I don't want to spend half my school year in a class that I really have no interest in.
**F:** Yeah, me neither!
**M:** And anyway, I just don't like the slower pace of the semester system.
**F:** I'm with you on that.
**M:** I like taking more classes in a shorter time. I feel like I learn more when I'm presented with such a wide variety of information. I know I'll just get bored if I'm forced to take a class for a whole semester.

### Prompt

The man expresses his opinion about the announcement described in the article. Briefly summarize the proposal. Then state his opinion about the announcement and explain the reasons he gives for holding that opinion.

### Announcement Notes

Proposal: _quarter sys. → semester sys._

- ↑ class time = ↑ learning
- reduce school costs

### Conversation Notes

Speaker's opinion: _man opposes_

- wants to finish req. courses quickly
- faster pace → focus better & less bored

 **Response**

The university proposes to change from the quarter to the semester system. A study shows that doing so could decrease costs and improve learning efficiency. The man disapproves of the proposal. One reason is that he wants to complete the required courses more quickly. Another reason is that he prefers a faster learning pace, which involves taking fewer classes over less time. He feels he learns more when he can focus his attention for a shorter period.

# TASK 4

## Model Answer

### PASSAGE

**Teen Obesity in the United States**

Over the past three decades, the number of obese children in the United States has more than doubled. These obesity rates are even higher among children from poor families. However, there are a number of ways that communities can work together to help reduce the alarmingly high rates of childhood obesity in the U.S.

### LECTURE

Today I'd like to talk about two consequences of the teen obesity problem in the U.S. These consequences are so severe that Americans need to spend time and money trying to prevent teen obesity through projects such as building more parks in poor neighborhoods.

The worst consequence of teen obesity is an increased risk for disease from a young age. People who are obese are more likely to develop a number of serious health conditions, including heart disease, diabetes, stroke, and cancer. Communities should try to prevent these serious health problems for their citizens and workforce by educating young people about the health risks associated with obesity.

Another reason that communities must work to reduce teen obesity is that the treatment of obesity-related diseases is expensive. Some experts estimate that treating obesity-related diseases in the U.S. costs nearly 200 billion dollars per year. The result is higher insurance costs and higher taxes for everyone.

### Prompt

Using the professor's examples, explain two consequences of teen obesity in the United States.

**Passage Notes**

Main Idea: *children obesity rate ↑,*

*esp. children from poor fam.*

- *multiple sol. to reduce children obesity rate*

**Lecture Notes**

Topic: *2 consequences of teen obesity*

Example 1: *increased risk for disease*

- Details: *heart disease, diabetes, stroke*

Example 2: *health care costs ↑*

- Details: *obesity → $200 billion/yr.*

 **Response**

The reading states that obesity rates among young people from poor families are rising steeply. The lecture outlines two consequences of these increasing obesity rates. First, the lecture claims that obese young people risk developing obesity-related diseases, such as diabetes and cancer. Furthermore, the lecture points out that this issue leads to another consequence of teen obesity: the costly treatment of these obesity-related diseases.

# Task 5

**CONVERSATION**

**F:** I'm so nervous for my upcoming philosophy midterm exam.

**M:** Why's that? I've seen you studying, so you should be prepared.

**F:** The stuff we're learning about is really tough. I'm afraid I'm going to fail the exam.

**M:** Have you thought about starting a study group? Maybe working with other people will make the information easier to understand.

**F:** That might work. But I don't really know that many people in the class.

**M:** Well, you could just ask some people at the end of your next lecture. Or I could help you study.

**F:** Oh, really? You could help me?

**M:** Yeah, I took the class last year from another instructor. You could review my notes.

**F:** That'd be great, as long as your instructor covered the same material as my instructor. And do you have time to help me out? I know you're pretty busy.

**M:** I'm pretty sure I can find time.

**F:** Female Student / **M:** Male Student

## Conversation Notes

Speaker's problem: _____

- Solution 1: _____

- Solution 2: _____

> **Prompt**
> Briefly summarize the problem the speakers are discussing. Then state which of the two solutions from the conversation you would recommend. Explain the reasons for your recommendation.

Preparation Time 00:00:20
Response Time 00:01:00

Use your 20 seconds of "Preparation Time" to organize your notes and prepare for your response.

**Preparation Notes**

Preferred solution: _____

- Reason 1: _____

- Reason 2: _____

Write your response on the lines below. Then **say your response aloud**, making sure that you can deliver your response in 1 minute.

**Response**

_____
_____
_____
_____
_____
_____
_____
_____
_____
_____

# TASK 6

**LECTURE**

### Ink-and-Wash Painting

Ink-and-wash painting is a practice from East Asia. Paintings are done using black ink lines and shading on silk or paper. The style started in China during the 7th century. Later, it spread to Korea and Japan.

Ink-and-wash painters usually illustrate landscapes, animals, and flowers. But these artists don't simply copy an object. Instead, they use lines to try to reveal the spirit of the subject. For example, when painting a cat, an ink-and-wash artist would try to illustrate the cat's mood and personality more than its physical appearance.

Now let's talk about ink-and-wash artists' technique. Artists often rely on shading to add detail and realism to their works. Hence, ink-and-wash painters can achieve endless varieties of shading by changing how much pressure and ink they use in each brushstroke.

**Lecture Notes**

Main Idea: _____

Subtopic 1: _____

- Details: _____

_____

Subtopic 2: _____

- Details: _____

_____

> **Prompt**
> Using points and examples from the lecture, explain the concepts behind ink-and-wash painting.

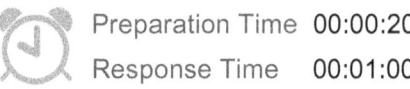

Preparation Time 00:00:20
Response Time 00:01:00

Use your 20 seconds of "Preparation Time" to organize your notes and prepare for your response.

Write your response on the lines below. Then **say your response aloud**, making sure that you can deliver your response in 1 minute.

**Response**

_____
_____
_____
_____
_____
_____
_____
_____
_____
_____

# Task 5

### Model Answer

**CONVERSATION**

**F:** I'm so nervous for my upcoming philosophy midterm exam.
**M:** Why's that? I've seen you studying, so you should be prepared.
**F:** The stuff we're learning about is really tough. I'm afraid I'm going to fail the exam.
**M:** Have you thought about starting a study group? Maybe working with other people will make the information easier to understand.
**F:** That might work. But I don't really know that many people in the class.
**M:** Well, you could just ask some people at the end of your next lecture. Or I could help you study.
**F:** Oh, really? You could help me?
**M:** Yeah, I took the class last year from another instructor. You could review my notes.
**F:** That'd be great, as long as your instructor covered the same material as my instructor. And do you have time to help me out? I know you're pretty busy.
**M:** I'm pretty sure I can find time.

**Prompt**

Briefly summarize the problem the speakers are discussing. Then state which of the two solutions from the conversation you would recommend. Explain the reasons for your recommendation.

## Conversation Notes

Speaker's problem: _woman worried abt. failing phil. midterm exam_

- Solution 1: _start a study group_
- Solution 2: _1-on-1 help from man_

## Preparation Notes

Preferred solution: _1-on-1 help from man_

- Reason 1: _private help better_
- Reason 2: _get started sooner_

### Response

Although she has studied, the woman is afraid of failing a philosophy midterm exam. The man suggests starting a study group. However, she says that will be difficult because she doesn't know many people in the class. He also offers to help her review. I believe she should study with the man. This will provide one-on-one support. Furthermore, studying with him will be quicker and easier than organizing a study group.

# Task 6

## Model Answer

### LECTURE

**Ink-and-Wash Painting**

*Ink-and-wash painting is a practice from East Asia. Paintings are done using black ink lines and shading on silk or paper. The style started in China during the seventh century. Later, it spread to Korea and Japan.*

*Ink-and-wash painters usually illustrate landscapes, animals, and flowers. But these artists don't simply copy an object. Instead, they use lines to try to reveal the spirit of the subject. For example, when painting a cat, an ink-and-wash artist would try to illustrate the cat's mood and personality more than its physical appearance.*

*Now let's talk about ink-and-wash artists' technique. Artists often rely on shading to add detail and realism to their works. Hence, ink-and-wash painters can achieve endless varieties of shading by changing how much pressure and ink they use in each brushstroke.*

### Prompt

Using points and examples from the lecture, explain the concepts behind ink-and-wash painting.

## Lecture Notes

Main Idea: *ink-and-wash painting (Asian)*

Subtopic 1: *capture spirit*

- Details: *paint nature, not realistic*

    *focus on mood, personality*

Subtopic 2: *technique → shading*

- Details: *variety from amount of pressure/ink*

 **Response**

The professor explains that ink-and-wash painting is a style of art that originated in China. The first ink-and-wash paintings are from the 7th century, and the technique involves using black ink on paper or silk. Instead of making a realistic depiction of something, the artist tries to capture its spirit. The artists do so by including a wide variety of shadings, using different pressures and amount of ink to add complexity to the painting.

# TASK 1

> **Prompt**
> Talk about a place where you feel relaxed. Describe it and explain why it is relaxing. Use specific reasons and examples to support your answer.

Preparation Time 00:00:15
Response Time 00:00:45

**Notes**

One place where I feel relaxed is _____

■ _____

■ _____

**Response**

_____
_____
_____
_____
_____
_____
_____
_____
_____
_____

# Task 2

**Prompt**

Most universities use the grading system. However, at some universities professors issue written reports describing students' work instead of issuing grades. Which grading method do you prefer and why? Use details and reasons to support your answer.

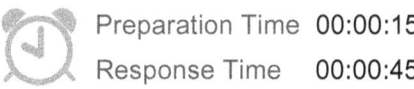

Preparation Time 00:00:15
Response Time 00:00:45

## Notes

I think universities should use (**a grading system / written reports**) to measure student progress.

- _____
- _____

## Response

_____
_____
_____
_____
_____
_____
_____
_____
_____

# TASK 1

## Model Answer

**Prompt**
Talk about a place where you feel relaxed. Describe it and explain why it is relaxing. Use specific reasons and examples to support your answer.

### Notes

One place where I feel relaxed is ___the beach___

- _friends → socialize, few worries_
- _ocean → waves, surf, swim_

 **Response**

One place where I feel relaxed is the beach. I find the beach so relaxing because it's often where my friends and I hang out. When I'm talking with my friends under the warm sun and the cool ocean breeze, my worries always disappear. Also, I enjoy ocean-related activities, such as swimming and surfing. I've often lost track of time relaxing on my surfboard and watching the waves pass by me.

# Task 2

## Model Answer

**Prompt**

Most universities use the grading system. However, at some universities professors issue written reports describing students' work instead of issuing grades. Which grading method do you prefer and why? Use details and reasons to support your answer.

### Notes

I think universities should use (**a grading system** / *__written reports__*) to measure student progress.

- *show improvement over time*

- *reflect attitude*

### Response

Although some students may prefer receiving grades, I believe written reports may evaluate students more accurately. For example, a report can explain a student's improvement over time. Grades may not reflect this. Furthermore, written reports can discuss a student's attitude and level of participation. This written information can be a useful resource that shows potential employers if a student is a capable candidate for a job.

# Task 3

**UNIVERSITY ANNOUNCEMENT**

### New Recreation Center

This summer, the old recreation center will be torn down, and a new recreation center will be built in its place. The center will offer new weight machines, a basketball court, and a pool. Student fees are expected to increase only slightly to cover the costs.

### Announcement Notes

Proposal: _____

- _____
- _____

**CONVERSATION**

**M:** I'm so glad that they're building a new recreation center.

**F:** I read about that. Why are you excited for the new center?

**M:** The old rec center is a wreck! It's old and falling apart.

**F:** I've definitely noticed that.

**M:** And the few weight machines that still work are ancient. They sound like they're going to break every time I use them.

**F:** Oh, I didn't realize it was that bad.

**M:** Plus the basketball court needs a lot of repairs. One of the basketball hoops is visibly crooked!

**M:** Male Student / **F:** Female Student

### Conversation Notes

Speaker's opinion: _____

- _____
- _____

> **Prompt**
> The man expresses his opinion about the proposal described in the article. Briefly summarize the proposal. Then state his opinion about the proposal and explain the reasons he gives for holding that opinion.

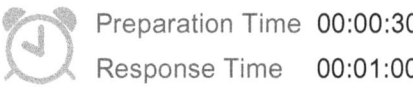

Preparation Time  00:00:30
Response Time     00:01:00

Use your 30 seconds of "Preparation Time" to organize your notes and prepare for your response.

Write your response on the lines below. Then **say your response aloud**, making sure that you can deliver your response in 1 minute.

### Response

_____

_____

_____

_____

_____

_____

_____

_____

_____

# Task 4

## PASSAGE

### Blood

Everyone knows that animals cannot live without blood. However, few people can explain what makes blood so important. In fact, blood is mostly water. Blood also includes blood cells, proteins, and sugars. Blood *circulates*, or travels in a circuit, through the body, removing waste products and delivering oxygen and nutrients where they are needed.

### Passage Notes

Main Idea: _____

- _____

- _____

## LECTURE

Now I'd like to talk about something mentioned briefly in the passage: blood cells. Human blood contains two types of blood cells called red blood cells and white blood cells.

There are more red blood cells than white blood cells, and red blood cells give blood its red color. The primary functions of red blood cells are to remove carbon dioxide from the circulatory system and to transport oxygen to where the body needs it.

White blood cells act like the body's bodyguards. These cells detect when the body is under attack from viruses or infections. Once they have located a potentially harmful invader, they attack it and prevent it from causing the body further harm.

### Lecture Notes

Topic: _____

Example 1: _____

- Details: _____

Example 2: _____

- Details: _____

> **Prompt**
> Using information from the passage and the lecture, explain the functions of blood cells in the human body.

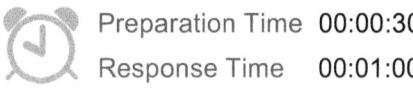

Preparation Time  00:00:30
Response Time    00:01:00

Use your 30 seconds of "Preparation Time" to organize your notes and prepare for your response.

Write your response on the lines below. Then **say your response aloud**, making sure that you can deliver your response in 1 minute.

**Response**

_____
_____
_____
_____
_____
_____
_____
_____
_____
_____

# Task 3

## Model Answer

### UNIVERSITY ANNOUNCEMENT

**New Recreation Center**

This summer, the old recreation center will be torn down, and a new recreation center will be built in its place. The center will offer new weight machines, a basketball court, and a pool. Student fees are expected to increase only slightly to cover the costs.

### CONVERSATION

**M:** I'm so glad that they're building a new recreation center.
**F:** I read about that. Why are you excited for the new center?
**M:** The old rec center is a wreck! It's old and falling apart.
**F:** I've definitely noticed that.
**M:** And the few weight machines that still work are ancient. They sound like they're going to break every time I use them.
**F:** Oh, I didn't realize it was that bad.
**M:** Plus the basketball court needs a lot of repairs. One of the basketball hoops is visibly crooked!

### Prompt

The man expresses his opinion about the proposal described in the article. Briefly summarize the proposal. Then state his opinion about the proposal and explain the reasons he gives for holding that opinion.

**Announcement Notes**

Proposal: _build new rec. center_

- _new workout/sport equip._
- _fee will ↑_

**Conversation Notes**

Speaker's opinion: _man supports_

- _old rec-center falling apart_
- _needs new weights & b-ball court_

 **Response**

The university announced that it will build a new recreation center. Student fees will go up only a small amount to cover the costs. The man supports the plan. One reason is that the original center is old and in poor condition. A second reason is that the equipment is old, and the basketball court needs repair work.

# TASK 4

## Model Answer

### PASSAGE

**Blood**

Everyone knows that animals cannot live without blood. However, few people can explain what makes blood so important. In fact, blood is mostly water. Blood also includes blood cells, proteins, and sugars. Blood *circulates*, or travels in a circuit, through the body, removing waste products and delivering oxygen and nutrients where they are needed.

### LECTURE

*Now I'd like to talk about something mentioned briefly in the passage: blood cells. Human blood contains two types of blood cells called red blood cells and white blood cells.*

*There are more red blood cells than white blood cells, and red blood cells give blood its red color. The primary functions of red blood cells are to remove carbon dioxide from the circulatory system and to transport oxygen to where the body needs it.*

*White blood cells act like the body's bodyguards. These cells detect when the body is under attack from viruses or infections. Once they have located a potentially harmful invader, they attack it and prevent it from causing the body further harm.*

### Prompt

Using information from the passage and the lecture, explain the functions of blood cells in the human body.

**Passage Notes**

Main Idea: _why blood impt._

- water, cells, protein, sugar
- brings nutrients, removes waste

**Lecture Notes**

Topic: _types of blood cells_

Example 1: _red blood cells (RBC)_

- Details: _>WBC; take $CO_2$ out; $O_2$ to body_

Example 2: _white blood cells (WBC)_

- Details: _find threats to body, attack them_

The reading gives a basic description of blood, which is made of water, proteins, sugars, and cells. The lecture further describes blood by discussing the functions of red and white blood cells. Red blood cells travel around the body and remove unnecessary carbon dioxide. They also carry oxygen where it's needed. White blood cells act like the body's security system; they find and attack viruses and infections before the virus or infection can seriously damage the rest of the body.

# Task 5

**CONVERSATION**

**M:** I'm going to be late again for Statistics.

**F:** What's the reason this time?

**M:** The same reason as always: my job. An employee calls in sick; I have to cover for them, and it makes me late every time.

**F:** Is it going to get any better at your job?

**M:** I hope so. They're hiring new people.

**F:** You could always stand up to your boss and tell him that you can't cover any more of your coworkers' shifts. I'm sure if you talk to your boss, he'll be reasonable and understand your situation.

**M:** That's true, but I'm afraid he'll just ignore me.

**F:** Hmmm… Well, another possibility is to talk to the professor. Maybe you could transfer to a class at a different time.

**M:** Isn't it too late in the quarter to switch classes?

**F:** I don't know, but it might be worth a try.

**M:** Male Student / **F:** Female Student

## Conversation Notes

Speaker's problem: _____

- Solution 1: _____

- Solution 2: _____

> **Prompt**
> Briefly summarize the problem the speakers are discussing. Then recommend a solution to the problem. Explain the reasons for your recommendation.

Preparation Time 00:00:20
Response Time 00:01:00

Use your 20 seconds of "Preparation Time" to organize your notes and prepare for your response.

**Preparation Notes**

Preferred solution: _____

- Reason 1: _____

- Reason 2: _____

Write your response on the lines below. Then **say your response aloud**, making sure that you can deliver your response in 1 minute.

**Response**

_____
_____
_____
_____
_____
_____
_____
_____
_____
_____

# Task 6

**ACTUAL PRACTICE 3**

**LECTURE**

### Eudora Welty

Writer Eudora Welty was an American short story writer and a novelist. In 1973, she was awarded the Pulitzer Prize in Fiction. Welty was also famous for discussing the process of writing fiction. Let's look at two of her suggestions to other writers.

One suggestion she offers writers is to create a sense of place in their writing, which includes describing the unique characteristics of a setting. Because locations are often associated with particular cultures, traditions, and emotions, creating a sense of place can help establish the tone of a story and make it seem real.

Another suggestion Welty offers writers is to take risks in their writing. One way she takes risks is by mixing influences from different times and cultures. For example, many of her stories are set in 20th century America, but they borrow plot elements from myths and legends. This mixing of reality and fantasy often gives Welty's stories a unique, dream-like quality.

**Lecture Notes**

Main Idea: _____

Subtopic 1: _____

- Details: _____

_____

Subtopic 2: _____

- Details: _____

_____

> **Prompt**
> Using points and examples from the lecture, explain Eudora Welty's suggestions to writers.

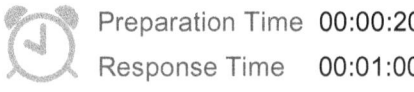

Preparation Time  00:00:20
Response Time    00:01:00

Use your 20 seconds of "Preparation Time" to organize your notes and prepare for your response.

Write your response on the lines below. Then **say your response aloud**, making sure that you can deliver your response in 1 minute.

**Response**

___
___
___
___
___
___
___
___
___

# TASK 5

## Model Answer

### CONVERSATION

**M:** I'm going to be late again for Statistics.
**F:** What's the reason this time?
**M:** The same reason as always: my job. An employee calls in sick; I have to cover for them, and it makes me late every time.
**F:** Is it going to get any better at your job?
**M:** I hope so. They're hiring new people.
**F:** You could always stand up to your boss and tell him that you can't cover any more of your coworkers' shifts. I'm sure if you talk to your boss, he'll be reasonable and understand your situation.
**M:** That's true, but I'm afraid he'll just ignore me.
**F:** Hmmm... Well, another possibility is to talk to the professor. Maybe you could transfer to a class at a different time.
**M:** Isn't it too late in the quarter to switch classes?
**F:** I don't know, but it might be worth a try.

### Prompt

Briefly summarize the problem the speakers are discussing. Then recommend a solution to the problem. Explain the reasons for your recommendation.

### Conversation Notes

Speaker's problem: _man late for class b/c of his job_

- Solution 1: _talk to boss_
- Solution 2: _talk to prof. → switch class to another time_

### Preparation Notes

Preferred solution: _talk to prof._

- Reason 1: _may be able to switch classes_
- Reason 2: _boss → hiring more ppl._

### Response

The man's problem is that his job causes him to be late for his class. The woman suggests that he could tell his boss that he can't take other people's shifts anymore. She also suggests that he talk to the instructor about switching classes. I think he should speak to the professor. He may still be able to change classes at this point in the quarter. Furthermore, the man says that the boss is hiring more people, so things may improve without him confronting his boss.

# TASK 6

## Model Answer

### LECTURE

**Eudora Welty**

Writer Eudora Welty was an American short story writer and a novelist. In 1973, she was awarded the Pulitzer Prize in Fiction. Welty was also famous for discussing the process of writing fiction. Let's look at two of her suggestions to other writers.

One suggestion she offers writers is to create a sense of place in their writing, which includes describing the unique characteristics of a setting. Because locations are often associated with particular cultures, traditions, and emotions, creating a sense of place can help establish the tone of a story and make it seem real.

Another suggestion Welty offers writers is to take risks in their writing. One way she takes risks is by mixing influences from different times and cultures. For example, many of her stories are set in 20th century America, but they borrow plot elements from myths and legends. This mixing of reality and fantasy often gives Welty's stories a unique, dream-like quality.

### Prompt

Using points and examples from the lecture, explain Eudora Welty's suggestions to writers.

## Lecture Notes

Main Idea: _E. Welty → won Pulitzer in 1973; wrote abt. writing process_

Subtopic 1: _create a sense of place_

- Details: _conveys culture, emo., story's tone_

Subtopic 2: _take risks_

- Details: _she mixes reality & fantasy_

 **Response**

The professor discusses Eudora Welty's points on the process of writing. Welty was an award-winning author, and she often gave suggestions about how to write well. One suggestion she gives writers is to develop a sense of specific location in their fiction. By doing so, writers can convey things such as culture and emotion. They can also set the tone of the story by describing the special features of the story's setting. Welty also encourages writers to take risks when writing. One way she takes risks is by mixing mythology with modern settings. As a result, Welty's stories are both realistic and fantasy-like.

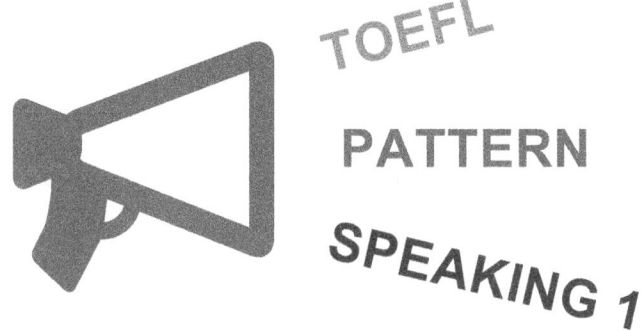

# CHAPTER 8

# Actual Test

## TASK 1

**Prompt**

Describe a hobby or an activity that you enjoy doing. Include specific reasons and examples in your response.

Preparation Time 00:00:15
Response Time 00:00:45

**Notes**

**Response**

## ACTUAL TEST

## TASK 2

**Prompt**

Some people like being self-employed. Others prefer working for someone else. Which do you prefer? Support your answer with reasons.

Preparation Time  00:00:15
Response Time  00:00:45

**Notes**

**Response**

# TASK 3

### UNIVERSITY ANNOUNCEMENT

**New Health Center**

The university will build a new health center next year. The current center is too small for the ever-growing student population. Furthermore, the medical equipment in the current center needs to be updated. The new center will be equipped with the latest medical equipment. The student tuition will be increased by 100 dollars annually to pay for the center.

### CONVERSATION

**M:** I hate for tuition to go up, but I think the new health center will be worth the money!

**F:** Oh yeah, I think so, too!

**M:** I went there when I sprained my ankle. It's so small that I had to wait outside the door because it was so packed with people. So I'm definitely looking forward to having larger facilities.

**F:** I know what you mean. I've seen it get like that sometimes.

**M:** And the new equipment will be great. When I needed to get an X-ray, the X-ray machine wasn't even working. So I had to spend a lot of money at a clinic off campus. The extra tuition will be justified if all the new equipment works.

*M: Male Student / F: Female Student*

**Notes**

_____
_____
_____
_____
_____
_____
_____
_____

## ACTUAL TEST

> **Prompt**
> The man expresses his opinion about the plan described in the announcement. Briefly summarize the plan. Then state his opinion about the plan and explain his reasons for holding that opinion.

Preparation Time 00:00:30
Response Time 00:01:00

### Response

# TASK 4

## PASSAGE

### Extinction Event

Many scientists describe an *extinction event* as a period when a large proportion of life on Earth suddenly dies off. In the past 500 million years, there have been five extinction events. It takes life millions of years to recover from an extinction event.

## LECTURE

Now that you know what an extinction event is, let's look at a couple of examples.

About 250 million years ago, the Permian-Triassic extinction event led to the extinction of over 90 percent of marine species and 70 percent of land-dwelling species. This event likely occurred when gradual environmental changes were followed by a global catastrophe, such as volcanic eruptions or meteor impacts.

The most recent extinction event occurred about 65 million years ago, and it's called the Cretaceous-Paleogene event. It likely occurred when a large meteor collided with Earth. The collision resulted in environmental changes that killed up to 75 percent of Earth's plant and animal species.

**Notes**

## ACTUAL TEST

**Prompt**
Using the instructor's examples, describe the two extinction events that occurred in the past.

Preparation Time 00:00:30
Response Time 00:01:00

**Response**

# TASK 5

**CONVERSATION**

**M:** Hey, Sarah. I really need your help.

**F:** Of course, David. What seems to be the problem?

**M:** I can't find a studio apartment anywhere near campus, and school starts soon. What should I do?

**F:** Have you tried checking for available apartments in the housing office? Listings come in daily.

**M:** I checked last week, but I didn't see anything that was in my price range.

**F:** Hmm… You could check again. But I know of a room in a house that might be available. It's a big room with a separate bathroom, and it's definitely cheaper than a studio apartment. Even though you'd have to share a kitchen with other residents, I think you'd like the room.

**M:** Thanks. I'd rather have a place all to myself, but I'll certainly consider sharing if necessary.

**M:** Male Student / **F:** Female Student

**Notes**

## ACTUAL TEST

**Prompt**

Briefly summarize the problem the speakers are discussing. Then state which of the two solutions from the conversation you would recommend. Explain the reasons for your recommendation.

Preparation Time 00:00:20
Response Time 00:01:00

**Response**

# TASK 6

**LECTURE**

### Health Care in the United States

One of the largest challenges faced by any developed country is making sure that every individual has access to health care. In the United States, two programs that provide health care to many individuals are Medicare and Medicaid.

Medicare provides medical insurance primarily to people over the age of 65, but young disabled people may also receive it. To receive Medicare, one must meet many qualifications and pay a monthly fee plus small additional fees for hospital visits.

Medicaid provides the funding for medical assistance to low-income individuals. Because local and state governments run Medicaid, the qualification for receiving Medicaid is different from location to location. For example, some recipients of Medicaid must pay a small monthly fee while others may receive Medicaid for free.

**Notes**

## ACTUAL TEST

**Prompt**

Using points and examples from the lecture, explain how Medicare and Medicaid contribute to health care in the United States.

Preparation Time  00:00:20
Response Time    00:01:00

**Response**

# TASK 1

**ACTUAL TEST**

## Model Answer

**Prompt**

Describe a hobby or an activity that you enjoy doing. Include specific reasons and examples in your response.

**Notes**

hobby → riding bikes

1) great exercise → stay in shape

2) enjoy outdoor activity (near ocean)

 **Response**

An activity I really enjoy is bicycle riding. One reason is that it gives me a great workout and helps me stay in shape. Consequently, I always feel refreshed after a long bike ride. Another reason I enjoy cycling is that it's fun to be outdoors. I especially like to ride my bike by the ocean because it allows me to enjoy the scenery and the cool ocean breeze as I exercise.

## ACTUAL TEST — TASK 2

### Model Answer

**Prompt**

Some people like being self-employed. Others prefer working for someone else. Which do you prefer? Support your answer with reasons.

**Notes**

*prefer having employer*

1) employer → steady work

    self-employed → find own work, risk ↑

2) benefits → sick time, paid holidays

 **Response**

Some people like being self-employed, but I prefer having an employer. There are two main reasons for this. One reason is that I prefer steady work. When you're self-employed, you have to find your own jobs and projects. And if a self-employed person is unable to find work, they risk losing money. Another reason I like working for an employer is because of the benefits, such as sick leave and paid holidays.

# TASK 3

**ACTUAL TEST**

**Model Answer**

### UNIVERSITY ANNOUNCEMENT

**New Health Center**

The university will build a new health center next year. The current center is too small for the ever-growing student population. Furthermore, the medical equipment in the current center needs to be updated. The new center will be equipped with the latest medical equipment. The student tuition will be increased by 100 dollars annually to pay for the center.

### CONVERSATION

**M:** I hate for tuition to go up, but I think the new health center will be worth the money!

**F:** Oh yeah, I think so, too!

**M:** I went there when I sprained my ankle. It's so small that I had to wait outside the door because it was so packed with people. So I'm definitely looking forward to having larger facilities.

**F:** I know what you mean. I've seen it get like that sometimes.

**M:** And the new equipment will be great. When I needed to get an X-ray, the X-ray machine wasn't even working. So I had to spend a lot of money at a clinic off campus. The extra tuition will be justified if all the new equipment works.

### Prompt

The man expresses his opinion about the plan described in the announcement. Briefly summarize the plan. Then state his opinion about the plan and explain his reasons for holding that opinion.

### Notes

proposal → new health center, new equip.

opinion → man supports

    1) current clinic too small/crowded

    2) more tuition ok for new equip.

 **Response**

The university plans on building a larger clinic and updating the medical equipment. Although tuition will increase to cover costs, the man approves of the plan. The clinic was crowded when he used it and equipment wasn't working properly. He believes that the added tuition won't be too much of an issue because the increase in tuition will be less expensive than the price of medical services off campus.

# ACTUAL TEST — TASK 4

**Model Answer**

### PASSAGE

**Extinction Event**

Many scientists describe an extinction event as a period when a large proportion of life on Earth suddenly die off. In the past 500 million years, there have been five extinction events. It takes life millions of years to recover from an extinction event.

### LECTURE

Now that you know what an extinction event is, let's look at a couple of examples.

About 250 million years ago, the Permian-Triassic extinction event led to the extinction of over 90 percent of marine species and 70 percent of land-dwelling species. This event likely occurred when gradual environmental changes were followed by a global catastrophe, such as volcanic eruptions or meteor impacts.

The most recent extinction event occurred about 65 million years ago, and it's called the Cretaceous-Paleogene event. It likely occurred when a large meteor collided with Earth. The collision resulted in environmental changes that killed up to 75 percent of Earth's plant and animal species.

### Prompt

Using the instructor's examples, describe the two extinction events that occurred in the past.

### Notes

extinction event → most life dies suddenly

250 mil. yrs. ago event: env. changes + meteor = most life dies

65 mil. yrs. ago event: meteor impact → env. changes → most life dies

 **Response**

The reading discusses extinction events, which are periods when much of Earth's life suddenly dies. The lecture gives two examples of these events, both caused by environmental changes, meteor impacts, or a combination of the two. The first extinction event the professor talks about happened 250 million years ago. Most land- and ocean- dwelling species became extinct because of environmental changes and global disasters. Then, about 65 million years ago, most life on Earth disappeared during another extinction event, which probably occurred because of a meteor impact.

# TASK 5 — ACTUAL TEST

**Model Answer**

### CONVERSATION

**M:** Hey, Sarah. I really need your help.

**F:** Of course, David. What seems to be the problem?

**M:** I can't find a studio apartment anywhere near campus, and school starts soon. What should I do?

**F:** Have you tried checking for available apartments in the housing office? Listings come in daily.

**M:** I checked last week, but I didn't see anything that was in my price range.

**F:** Hmm… You could check again. But I know of a room in a house that might be available. It's a big room with a separate bathroom, and it's definitely cheaper than a studio apartment. Even though you'd have to share a kitchen with other residents, I think you'd like the room.

**M:** Thanks. I'd rather have a place all to myself, but I'll certainly consider sharing if necessary.

### Prompt

Briefly summarize the problem the speakers are discussing. Then state which of the two solutions from the conversation you would recommend. Explain the reasons for your recommendation.

### Notes

problem → man can't find apt.

sol. 1 → check housing center

sol. 2 → room w/ bath but share kitchen

preferred sol. → sol. 2 (friends ↑, cost ↓)

 **Response**

The man can't find a studio apartment, and school is starting soon. The woman suggests checking the student housing office. She also mentions that she might know where the man can rent a room that's similar to a studio apartment. Personally, I think he should consider the room that she mentioned. One reason is that he might like the room itself, and he may become friends with the other people who live there. Another reason is that the room is cheaper than a studio apartment, so he could save money if he chooses to live there.

# ACTUAL TEST — TASK 6

## Model Answer

### LECTURE

**Health Care in the United States**

One of the largest challenges faced by any developed country is making sure that every individual has access to health care. In the United States, two programs that provide health care to many individuals are Medicare and Medicaid.

Medicare provides medical insurance primarily to people over the age of 65, but young disabled people may also receive it. To receive Medicare, one must meet many qualifications and pay a monthly fee plus small additional fees for hospital visits.

Medicaid provides the funding for medical assistance to low-income individuals. Because local and state governments run Medicaid, the qualification for receiving Medicaid is different from location to location. For example, some recipients of Medicaid must pay a small monthly fee while others may receive Medicaid for free.

### Prompt

Using points and examples from the lecture, explain how Medicare and Medicaid contribute to health care in the United States.

### Notes

U.S. health care → Medicare & Medicaid

Medicare: for ppl. over 65, disabled ppl,; monthly fee + little $ for hosp. visit

Medicaid: for low-income ppl.; state to state → qual. diff. (ex. monthly fee/free)

### Response

The professor talks about the health care programs in the U.S. called Medicare and Medicaid. According to the lecture, Medicare gives health insurance to people over 65 as well as young people with disabilities. Those who get Medicare have to pay a monthly fee and pay extra for hospital visits. Medicaid helps low-income people afford health care. The requirements for Medicaid vary by state, so some recipients of Medicaid must pay a monthly fee while others don't.

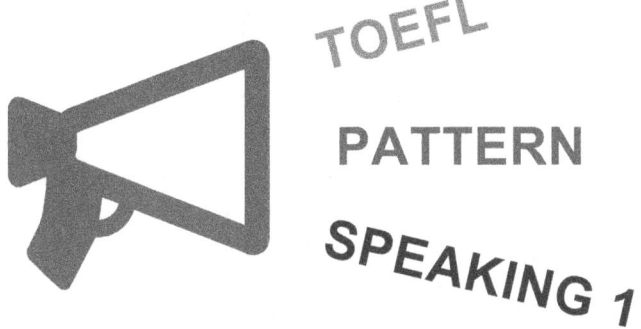

# APPENDIX

# Answer Key

▶ Note: All listed answers are examples; responses will vary.

# CHAPTER 1

p. 7

**PRACTICE 1** (*Answers will vary.*)

2) Modern Family          Top Gear
3) The Beatles            Queen
4) Harry Potter           Lord of the Rings
5) The Dark Knight        Star Wars
6) dog                    cat
7) sunny                  snowy
8) curious                happy

**PRACTICE 2** (*Answers will vary.*)

1) photo album w/ fam. pics.
2) fav. = comedy
3) the beach

p. 9

**PRACTICE 1** (*Answers will vary.*)

1) **Opinion**: photo album w/ fam. pics.
   **TS**: My most treasured possession is a large photo album with four generations of family photos.
2) **Op**: fav. = comedy
   **TS**: Although I enjoy films from every genre, my favorite type of movie to watch is usually comedy.
3) **Op**: the beach
   **TS**: When I have free time, my favorite place to visit is the beach.

p. 11

**PRACTICE 1** (*Answers will vary.*)

1) **TS**: My most treasured possession is a large photo album with four generations of family photos.
   ▶ **NOTES**
   **Reason 1**: tells my fam.'s story/history
   **Reason 2**: holds much emotional/sentimental value
2) **TS**: Although I enjoy films from every genre, my favorite type of movie to watch is usually comedy.
   ▶ **NOTES**
   **Reason 1**: fun to watch w/ friends
   **Reason 2**: laughter → relax/forget worries
3) **TS**: When I have free time, my favorite place to visit is the beach.
   ▶ **NOTES**
   **Reason 1**: enjoy relaxing in the Sun
   **Reason 2**: enjoy swimming/exercising in the ocean

p. 13

**PRACTICE 1** (*Answers will vary.*)

1) **Op**: trad. = Day of the Dead
   **TS**: One holiday from my home country of Mexico that I enjoy is the Day of the Dead.
   **Reason 1**: remember deceased fam.
   **Reason 2**: dress up, celebrate
   **Rs**: One holiday from my home country of Mexico that I enjoy is the Day of the Dead. This holiday is a time to celebrate one's deceased family members, and it's important to me for a couple of reasons. First, I use this holiday as an opportunity to remember my late grandmother. She helped raise me as a child, and she was always a positive influence. Second, this holiday gives me an opportunity to dress up and celebrate with living friends and family.

# CHAPTER 2

p. 29

**PRACTICE 1** (*Answers will vary.*)

2) I prefer having more than one career during my lifetime to having only one career.
3) I would rather live in a large city than live in a small town.
4) I prefer going to college right after high school to taking a break from my education.
5) I would rather choose work that I love but pays poorly than choose a high-paying, undesirable job.

**PRACTICE 2** (*Answers will vary.*)

1) typing an essay
2) following a schedule
3) learning abt. humanities

p. 31

**PRACTICE 1** (*Answers will vary.*)

1) **Preference**: typing an essay
   **TS**: Although some people prefer writing their essays by hand, I prefer typing them up on a computer for a number of reasons.
2) **Preference**: following a schedule
   **TS**: Some people feel restricted by daily schedules, but I actually prefer following a schedule to being spontaneous.
3) **Preference**: learning about humanities
   **TS**: While many of my peers enjoy learning about mathematics and the sciences, I prefer learning about the humanities, especially history and literature.

p. 33

**PRACTICE 1 (Answers will vary.)**

1) **TS**: Although some people prefer writing their essays by hand, I prefer typing them up on a computer for a number of reasons.
   ▸ **NOTES**
   **Reason 1**: type faster than write
   **Reason 2**: easier to edit, proofread

2) **TS**: Some people feel restricted by daily schedules, but I actually prefer following a schedule to being spontaneous.
   ▸ **NOTES**
   **Reason 1**: enjoy planning, structure
   **Reason 2**: always feel prepared

3) **TS**: While many of my peers enjoy learning about mathematics and the sciences, I prefer learning about the humanities, especially history and literature.
   ▸ **NOTES**
   **Reason 1**: hist. → understand events that led to present
   **Reason 2**: literature → see world from diff. perspectives

p. 35

**PRACTICE 1 (Answers will vary.)**

1) **Preference**: receiving help from professors
   **TS**: When I'm faced with a challenging concept or a confusing topic in school, I prefer to receive help from a professor or instructor for a number of reasons.
   **Reason 1**: their answers → reliably correct
   **Reason 2**: 1-on-1 interaction w/ instructor
   **Rs**: When I'm faced with a challenging concept in school, I prefer to receive help from a professor or an instructor. Firstly, I prefer asking my instructors for help because I'm confident that they'll give me correct answers to my questions. All my professors are experts in their areas of study, so I know their responses are reliable. Moreover, asking my instructors questions will help me get to know them. Building these relationships can be helpful when seeking teacher recommendations or internships later on.

## CHAPTER 3

p. 51

**PRACTICE 1 (Answers will vary.)**
**Proposal**: build new parking lot (tuition ↑ $100)
**Reason 1**: too many students for current lot
**Reason 2**: new location = less walking for students

p. 53

**PRACTICE 1 (Answers will vary.)**
**Opinion**: man opposes
**Reason 1**: lot unnecessary, bad location
**Reason 2**: can't afford tuition ↑

p. 55

**PRACTICE 1 (Answers will vary.)**

1) **From Notes → Proposal**: build new parking lot (tuition ↑ $100)
2) **From Notes → Opinion**: man opposes
3) **From Notes → Reason 1**: lot unnecessary, bad location
   **Reason 2**: can't afford increase to tuition

p. 57

**PRACTICE 1 (Answers will vary.)**
**Rs**: The announcement states that the university will raise student tuition by 100 dollars next year in order to build a new parking lot. The man is opposed to this plan. For one, he believes that the parking lot is unnecessary because most students don't have cars. Additionally, he doesn't appreciate the fact that the school intends to build the lot where he often eats lunch. Finally, he claims that he can't afford the tuition increase that would accompany the construction project.

## CHAPTER 4

p. 77

**PRACTICE 1 (Answers will vary.)**
**Main Idea**: Harlem Renaissance (period of much cultural productivity by African-Am.)
**Details**: 1920s-1930s; mostly in Harlem, NY (also elsewhere in U.S.)

p. 79

**PRACTICE 1 (Answers will vary.)**
**Topic**:
**Example 1**: new blues/jazz during Harlem Ren.
**Details**: caused white composers to become interested in/ influenced by African-Am. music
**Example 2**: new authors, poets, editors during Harlem Ren.
**Details**: realistic portrayal of African-Am. lives; writing about good & bad events

p. 81

**PRACTICE 1 (Answers will vary.)**

1) **From Notes → Main Idea**: Harlem Renaissance (period of cultural productivity by African Americans)

2) **From Notes → Example 1**: new African-Am. blues/jazz musicians
   **Example 2**: new writers, editors, poets
3) **From Notes → Details**: white composers became influenced by African-Am. music realistic portrayal of African-Am. lives; writing about good and bad events

p. 83

**PRACTICE 1** (*Answers will vary.*)

**Rs**: According to the passage, the Harlem Renaissance was a period during the 1920s and 1930s when African-American culture and publishing flourished. During the Harlem Renaissance, many African-American musicians began testing new forms of jazz and blues. These new styles interested many white composers who used these influences in their own music. Furthermore, many African-American writers during Harlem Renaissance were inspired to give realistic depictions of African-American life. Thus, these writers depicted the bad and the good aspects to daily life.

## CHAPTER 5

p. 103

**PRACTICE 1** (*Answers will vary.*)
▶ **CONVERSATION NOTES**
**Problem**: man can't afford tuition
   **Solution 1**: get student loan
   **Solution 2**: apply for scholarships

p. 105

**PRACTICE 1** (*Answers will vary.*)
1) **From Notes → Problem**: man can't afford tuition
2) **Preferred solution**: get student loan
3) **Reason 1**: receive $ immediately
   **Reason 2**: guaranteed to get $

p. 107

**PRACTICE 1** (*Answers will vary.*)

**Rs**: In the conversation, the man's problem is that he doesn't have enough money to pay for tuition next quarter. In my opinion, the man should take out a student loan. The first reason I prefer this solution is that the money from a student loan would be available immediately. Furthermore, he's guaranteed to receive money from a student loan, whereas there's a good chance that he would be denied a scholarship.

## CHAPTER 6

p. 127

**PRACTICE 1** (*Answers will vary.*)
▶ **LECTURE NOTES**
**Main Idea**: animal migration (for food, climate, breeding)
**Subtopic 1**: humpbacks 25,000-km trip
**Details**: summer = cold polar water for feeding, winter = warm waters for breeding
**Subtopic 2**: salmon migration
**Details**: grow in ocean, swim upstream to breed; most die

p. 129

**PRACTICE 1**
1) **From Notes → Main Idea**: animal migration (for food, climate, breeding)
2) **From Notes → Subtopic 1**: humpbacks migrate 25,000 km; summer = cold polar water for feeding, winter = warm waters for breeding
3) **From Notes → Subtopic 1**: salmon grow in ocean, migrate upstream to breed; most die

p. 131

**PRACTICE 1** (*Answers will vary.*)

**Rs**: According to the lecture, many animals migrate to access more food, a better climate, or safe breeding grounds. For example, humpback whales migrate to polar waters each summer in order to access the plentiful food there. Then, in winter, the whales swim toward the equator to breed in warm water. Additionally, the lecture mentions salmon migrations, which begin in the ocean. When salmon are fully grown, they swim upstream in rivers to access their breeding grounds. The journey is so difficult that most salmon die during the migration.